Just
Christians Fight

A Scriptural Inquiry

Mennonite Central Committee

THE MENNONITE CENTRAL COMMITTEE

Representing the following groups in the United States:

The Mennonite Church, The General Conference of the Mennonite Church of North America, The Mennonite Brethren, The Old Order Amish Mennonites, The Church of God in Christ (Mennonite), The Central Conference of Mennonites, The Conservative Amish Mennonites, The Evangelical Mennonite Brethren, The Krimmer Mennonite Brethren, The Brethren in Christ.

MEMBERS: P. C. Hiebert, Sterling, Kans.; P. H. Unruh, Goessel, Kansas; Orie O. Miller, Akron, Pa.; Harold S. Bender, Goshen, Ind.; Allen Yoder, Goshen, Ind.; Jesse W. Hoover, Nappanee, Ind.; S. C. Yoder, Goshen, Ind.; Henry F. Garber, Mt. Joy, Pa.; Irwin W. Bauman, Bluffton, Ohio; Frank H. Wenger, Moundridge, Kansas; P. G. Schultz, Evergreen Park, Ill.; H. E. Bertsche, Gridley, Ill.; Elmer G. Swartzendruber, Wellman, Iowa; Eli J. Bontrager, Shipshewana, Ind.; David V. Wiebe, Hillsboro, Kans.; J. A. Huffman, Marion, Ind.

OFFICERS: P. C. Hiebert, Sterling, Kansas, *Chairman;* P. H. Unruh, Goessel, Kansas, *Vice-Chairman;* Orie O. Miller, Akron, Pa., *Secretary-Treasurer;* Harold S. Bender, Goshen, Indiana, *Asst. Sec'y.;* Allen Yoder, Goshen, Indiana, *Executive Committee.*

PEACE SECTION: H. S. Bender, *Chairman;* Jesse W. Hoover, Nappanee, Indiana, *Secretary;* P. C. Hiebert, O. O. Miller, Ernest Bohn, Souderton, Pa.

EDITORIAL COMMITTEE FOR "MUST CHRISTIANS FIGHT": Harold S. Bender, Goshen, Ind.; Jesse W. Hoover, Nappanee, Ind.; Edward Yoder, Scottdale, Pa.; Ernest Bohn, Souderton, Pa.; S. F. Coffman, Vineland, Ontario; P. C. Hiebert, Sterling, Kansas; Shem Peachey, Springs, Pa.

PRICE PER COPY TWENTY CENTS.

MUST CHRISTIANS FIGHT

A Scriptural Inquiry

By

EDWARD YODER

in collaboration with

JESSE W. HOOVER AND HAROLD S. BENDER

Published by

THE MENNONITE CENTRAL COMMITTEE

Akron, Pennsylvania

1943

MUST CHRISTIANS FIGHT?

CONTENTS

FIFTY-SIX QUESTIONS AND ANSWERS

Introduction

In recent times a surprisingly large volume of articles, pamphlets, and even books have been published by "fundamentalist" authors which attempt to prove on scriptural grounds that it is not only right for the Christian to take part in war, but that he *must* do so if he is to fulfil his Christian duty. Apparently the conscience of many an earnest believer has been troubled in regard to participation in the current war. Is it right for a Christian to take part in bloodshed? May he as a Christian lend his energy, money, mind, heart, and life to that which certainly seems on the surface to violate every basic principle of Christian living which the Bible teaches? How can he hate, kill, and destroy; how can he starve the helpless by blockades; how can he help buy the bombs that will rain down upon millions with sudden death and destruction from the skies; how can he take part in the deceptions and lying propaganda of modern war; in short how can he take part in or even consider all the fearsome evils which seem to be essential to war, but are in fact deliberate violations of the normal Christian ethical code which the Bible so plainly teaches and which he endeavors to practice in his daily, personal life? It is inevitable that a pure conscience should be deeply disturbed by these searching questions.

In the attempt to quiet these movings of conscience, a certain class of "fundamentalist" writers, using their authority and prestige as experienced and revered teachers of the Word, have attempted to prove that the Bible does not forbid warfare and that one may be a follower of Jesus and still participate in the current conflict. This attempt has often been undertaken in the course of Christian history; in fact it is the official position of the Roman Catholic Church and practically all Protestant bodies, and has been so for centuries; hence it is not strange that conservative Bible teachers should follow in their train. The astonishing thing is that the "fundamentalist" Bible teacher often should go far beyond this position and seek to lay a binding duty upon Christians to take part in war, and condemn those who teach Biblical nonresistance as false teachers and enemies of the Word of God. The Christian *must* fight, they say; he has no choice. Some even claim that wars are necessary, that this is God's way of dealing with the world's problems, and that governments are remiss in their duty when they do not wage war. In any case, we are instructed, a Christian must trust the state and obey the call to arms, and the nonresistant Christian who refuses this response is to be put outside the company of true believers. On this point it is sad to note that the "fundamentalists" are at times harsher and more intolerant toward the nonresistant position than writers and preachers of liberal or modernist persuasion.

Since there are several hundred thousand nonresistant Christians in America who hold themselves to be thoroughly sound, devout, and orthodox Bible-believing-and-obeying followers of Christ, many of whom are grieved, and some of whom are confused, by the attacks made on Biblical nonresistance by persons whom they have hitherto highly regarded, it seemed good and right that a clear Scriptural exposition of the nonresistant position should be made available, in which point by point the most common arguments of the opposition would be met. Those who sponsor this publication believe that the opposition arguments advanced on supposed Biblical grounds can be met, and that it is the duty of those who believe this to give their witness to Divine truth in regard to the Bible teaching on war, peace, and nonresistance, without surrendering one whit of the heavenly message.

The form of this booklet is intended to make the nonresistant witness as clear and direct as possible in terms of the current need. The arguments of the opposition, as set forth in 56 brief questions, each followed by scriptural answer, were derived from a careful digest of all the available published material treating the theme, over forty separate publications having been used for this purpose. The basic answers were prepared by an editorial committee, and then turned into a finished literary production by an author and two collaborators. The final draft of the manuscript was approved by a large number of leading bishops, preachers, and Bible teachers from all branches of the Mennonite Church and the Brethren in Christ. A detailed list of persons concerned in the preparation for publication of the booklet is printed on the inside of the front cover. The authors invite all those earnest Christians who are confused on the question as to whether a Christian must fight, or who may already have been convinced that the answer to such a question is yes, to seek afresh through the help of this booklet to discover God's holy will in regard to war, and having found it to obey the same with a pure conscience.

August 15, 1943   HAROLD S. BENDER

The Point of View of This Booklet

Many earnest Christians are greatly puzzled over the question: What is my duty as a Christian when my nation is at war? They believe the Bible to be the Word of God; they accept it as the Christian's guide for both his faith and his practice; they know it is their duty to obey its teachings. In all seriousness they ask, "What does the Bible really teach about war and nonresistance?"

When these conscientious believers inquire of orthodox and evangelical teachers of the Bible, they find wide disagreement as to what they think the Bible teaches about the Christian's duty in regard to war. It dismays them to find Bible teachers who claim alike to accept the whole Bible as the inspired Word of God but who nevertheless teach practically opposite views on the subjects of nonresistance and war. Some, they find, teach that according to the Scriptures the Christian must fight in defense of his country when the nation requires this service of him in a time of crisis, regardless of whether the individual has a conscience on the question or not. Others teach with equal emphasis and conviction that Christians, according to the Scriptures, must practice nonresistance and not consent to perform any service for the nation that involves the destruction of the life and property of other people, for such destruction involves the breaking of God's commands.

What shall the conscientious Christian do amid this conflicting teaching and confusing counsel? How can he know with any degree of certainty what it is that God requires of him when the doctors disagree so widely? In the following pages we shall seek to answer this question by considering the Scriptures as a whole from the standpoint of giving our loyalty to Jesus Christ as the Christian's supreme authority for faith and life.

In answering the questions at the heads of the following sections we hope to dispose of the objections that are commonly made against nonresistance as a Christian principle. This we purpose to do by turning the light of the simple Scripture teaching on this question and illuminating the darkened counsel that is being offered. The aim will be to exalt Jesus Christ and His authority for determining the Christian's faith and life, and to grasp the teaching of the Scriptures as a whole in relation to Christ. It is our

9

conviction that the Scriptures teach the principle of nonresistance, and that loyalty to Christ as our Lord requires us as His followers to take up the cross and follow Him in the way of love and nonresistance as well as in other teachings He gave (Matt. 16:24). We venture humbly to defend this position, and in doing so briefly set forth the Scriptural grounds on which nonresistant believers have based their teaching on this subject.

EDWARD YODER

The Scripture quotations used in the following pages have been taken uniformly from the American Standard (Revised) version published by Thomas Nelson and Sons, New York, N. Y.

MUST CHRISTIANS FIGHT?

A Scriptural Inquiry

1. WHAT IS BIBLICAL NONRESISTANCE?

The term "nonresistance" is apparently derived directly from the words of Jesus in Matthew 5:39, "I say unto you, Resist not him that is evil." The same idea is also expressed in other places in the Scriptures, where we find the words "Render to no man evil for evil," "Avenge not yourselves." All these Scriptures forbid Christians to pay back an aggressor in his own spirit and with his kind of action. (See Prov. 20:22; Rom. 12:17, 19; I Thes. 5:15; I Pet. 3:9).

Some Bible teachers say that neither the Scriptures nor Jesus by His own example gives a sanction to the passive, yielding, weak attitude toward wrongdoers which is implied in the term nonresistance.

This challenge reveals an imperfect understanding of what is meant by nonresistance in the Biblical sense. The term taken by itself is easily misleading, for its negative form does not suggest the true nature of the principle in question. The Christian is not commanded to be passive and unassertive in his attitude toward evil and sin and wrongdoing. He must resist the Devil (Jas. 4:7; I Pet. 5:9). He is required to contend or wrestle for the true faith once for all delivered to the saints (Jude 3). The right Scriptural attitude toward sin and unrighteousness is anything but passive, weak, yielding, or supine, as some mistakenly take the term nonresistance to suggest. Even toward those who do him wrong the Christian is not passive in attitude. To go a second mile with the man who asks for one mile is not negative but aggressive; it is a powerful kind of resistance. But it is not resisting evil men on their own low, unregenerate level of conduct. The nonresistant does not pay back the evildoer in his own coin. It is only in a limited sense that nonresistance is negative.

For his assault upon sin and evil, and for his reactions to those who do him wrong, the Christian has other weapons to use than mere earthly, carnal weapons. He has for his use spiritual weapons and spiritual armor (II Cor. 10:3-5; Eph. 6:10-18). He takes an aggressive attitude toward those who may wrong him, by praying for their conversion, by returning good deeds for their

11

evil deeds, by showing unfailing good will toward them under all circumstances (Matt. 5:44; Luke 6:28), by overcoming evil with good (Romans 12:21). He is ready to suffer personal injury and loss rather than to inflict these on another even in self defense (I Cor. 6:7). In other words, the nonresistant Christian, if he is a consistent follower of Jesus Christ, lives a life of devotion and spiritual power, a life that is active and aggressive in doing good to all men, a life such as enables him to meet evil men with weapons of superior power, and to overcome.

Nonresistance as defined above can arise only out of a heart that is filled with the love of God; it is the fruit of a life in which the Holy Spirit, which is the spirit of Christ, reigns. (I Thess. 3:12-15). This does not mean that all professed nonresistant people live lives filled with the power of the Spirit, and that there are no nominal nonresistant Christians, but rather that the ultimate effectiveness of nonresistance depends on the Spirit of God.

2. DOES THE BIBLE CONTAIN CONTRADICTORY TEACHINGS ON THE MATTER OF WAR AND NONRESISTANCE?

We have noted above that different Bible teachers do in fact teach opposite and contradictory things from the Bible on these subjects. From seeing this the superficial observer may become discouraged and conclude that the Bible contradicts itself, and that every teacher picks out from the Bible just that particular line of Scripture texts which he likes, and quotes those passages which support the position he prefers to take.

Such a despairing conclusion, however, cannot satisfy one who believes the Bible is throughout the inspired Word of God and constitutes a unity. If God is the original Author of the Scriptures as a whole, we must believe that the teachings contained in it are consistent with each other, if only we were once able to understand them rightly. It cannot be true that the God who inspired the Old Testament was a God of war and vengeance and held one standard of right and wrong, and that the God who inspired the New Testament is a God of love and forgiveness and held to a different standard which he adopted for the first time in 26-30 A.D. It is our task, therefore, as sincere believers in the Word of God, humbly to seek for the correct approach to the Scriptures, an approach which will enable us to see them as a unit and to interpret them in a manner that is consistent.

We hold that the Scriptures teach the principle of nonresistance as a rule of life for the Christian. Certain groups such as the Mennonites, Quakers, Brethren, and Brethren in Christ, have for

12

centuries believed this to be true and have tried to live by this principle at whatever cost was necessary for the adventure. There is evidence at hand too that there have been larger and smaller bodies of Christians in all the centuries since Christ who have been nonresistant in faith and practice, and that today they are scattered throughout all denominations. This fact is an added incentive for us to try to understand the Bible in its entirety and to grasp the full truth pertaining to war and nonresistance, so far as this may be possible for finite human minds.

3. WHERE SHOULD THE EARNEST CHRISTIAN BEGIN STUDYING THE BIBLE TO FIND OUT WHAT TO DO IN REGARD TO WAR?

How shall one search the Scriptures in honesty and candor for light on what the Christian should do in regard to war? It is not really necessary to be a theologian and a scholar in order to discover the teaching of the Scriptures on this subject. It is essential, however, that one take the position of a humble and sincere believer on the Lord Jesus Christ, and begins with experience of saving faith in Christ.

This simple believer rejoices in the salvation which Christ has purchased for him on Calvary's cross. He deeply loves the Lord Jesus Christ with all his heart. He has gladly accepted Christ not only as his Saviour but also as the Lord and King of his life. Without reservation he has made the all-out commitment, the unconditional pledge to yield his life into the hands of Jesus Christ. It is his intention to follow Christ, to bear the cross, and to walk in His ways, whatever the cost may be. He knows that salvation is found in no other name than that of Jesus, and that no other foundation can be laid. (I Cor. 3:11, and Acts 4:12).

Where now would be the most natural and the most logical place for this Christian believer to begin his study of the Bible in order to find out what he must do that he might follow the Master whom he loves and adores? Will it not be to the Gospels of the New Testament that contain the words of Jesus that he will go first? It is altogether right that he derive his first and fundamental knowledge of the life of Christ and of the teachings of Christ from these simple and revealing records.

Let us suppose then that as a simple and devout believer he reads the Gospels carefully over and over. From them he soon gets a rather definite impression of the spirit and life of the Master whom he is pledged to follow. He reads how this Master lived among men and how He dealt with people, and he observes the

13

manner of His life as a whole. In the Gospels he reads many simple and direct teachings of Jesus, as for example in the Sermon on the Mount. He needs no one to tell him that these teachings were meant by his Master to serve as his guide in the way of life; this he knows instinctively. If someone should come to him and try to convince him that Jesus did not really mean for His followers to act upon these teachings in all the relationships of life, private and otherwise, he would be surprised and perplexed. The Master's words and the spirit and manner in which He lived inevitably and irresistibly challenge him to follow in His footsteps.

This earnest believer will read some things in the Gospels which perhaps he cannot readily understand or explain. But the primary and fundamental picture of the Christ and the impression of His teachings on love, well-doing, forgiveness, purity, and so forth, he can never allow to be dimmed or blacked out by perplexing questions over isolated passages. The plain and direct teachings of the Gospels must be the platform on which he takes his stand as a follower of Christ.

Later on this follower of Christ will read other parts of the Bible. Some parts he will find to be plain and direct in form and in meaning, and these will frequently confirm and strengthen the impression of his Master which he has already gained from the Gospels. Other parts may be obscure to him, and some may even appear to conflict with the conception of his Saviour as he has learned to know Him from the Gospels. But he should not let himself be disturbed by this experience.

This will be the principle to which he must always hold firmly, that nothing which he reads in other parts of the Bible must be allowed to cancel out or refute for him the plain words of Jesus Christ Himself or what is said about Him in the Gospels. The earnest seeker need not be able to explain at once, for instance, why godly people in the Old Testament lived differently from the standard that Jesus proclaimed. Those are questions which he can study in the course of time and find explanations for them. But for knowing his duty as a follower of Christ, his Master and Lord is the supreme authority and what He taught is the rule to which he needs to hold fast. True, all the Scriptures are inspired and are profitable for use by the Christian; they can all contribute to his knowledge and understanding of God and of His divine work of redemption; and what has been said about the authority of Christ does not modify this.

If we are disciples of Jesus, pledged as Christians to follow

14

Him and to go forward in the way of the cross with Him, we must be like the humble believer we have imagined above. The Gospels of the New Testament must be the standard, the fundamental pattern for our faith and practice as Christians. The rest of the New Testament is in harmony with the Gospels, and the Christian accordingly takes the entire New Testament for his standard.

So we may repeat again that Christ is the supreme authority for the Christian's faith and life. All other rules, standards, authorities, patterns of life, precedents, and what not, must be brought into subjection to His authority for the Christian believer. Christ is the Head over all things to the Church (Eph. 1:20-22). It is sad to note that some who attack the nonresistant faith, very lightly ignore or explain away the supremacy of Jesus Christ. They appear to be quite ready to cancel out His teachings with something found elsewhere in the Bible, some other pattern or way of life which avoids the way of the cross.

4. WHY IS JESUS CHRIST THE SUPREME AUTHORITY FOR THE CHRISTIAN'S FAITH AND LIFE?

Let the Scriptures answer the question before us. After His resurrection from the dead Christ declared, "All authority hath been given unto me in heaven and on earth" (Matt 28:18). As the Risen Lord He has all authority to send out His followers to evangelize the nations and to teach them all the things which He has commanded them.

On the Mount of Transfiguration two prominent representatives of the Old Testament visited and talked with Christ. After these had vanished from sight, the voice of God spoke, "This is my beloved Son, hear ye him" (Mark 9:7). The marvelous scene on the Mount symbolized the fact that Christ and His authority have now superseded the Old Testament regime, and men henceforth are commanded to hear and obey Jesus only.

In the Old Testament God's revelation was partial and incomplete over a long period of time; the New Testament revelation was given to complete the revelation. In the opening words of the Epistle to the Hebrews we read, "God having of old time spoken unto the fathers in the prophets by divers portions and in divers manners, hath at the end of these days spoken unto us in his Son, whom he appointed heir of all things."

It is on the basis of these and other Scriptures (I Cor. 3:11, I Peter 2:21) that we hold that the Christian, one who has pledged himself to follow Christ, must look up to Him as his supreme

Lord and King. From His life, from His teachings as these are recorded in the New Testament, he takes the pattern for his own faith and practice. He cannot conceive of going elsewhere for the pattern for his faith and life without deserting his Master and being traitor to the One who has loved him and given Himself for his redemption, purchasing him with His own precious blood.

5. WHAT IS THE ESSENTIAL CHARACTER OF CHRIST AS POR-
   TRAYED IN THE NEW TESTAMENT? IS IT PEACEFUL AND
   NONRESISTANT OR WARLIKE?

The assertion is made by some, that the commonly accepted picture of Jesus as a weak, inoffensive, harmless soul, a picture attributed to the nonresistant, has been allowed to go unchallenged too long, and that it is not the New Testament picture.

It is, of course, incorrect to infer from the Gospels that Jesus was a weakling, a dreamy, impractical sort of person. His was in fact a forceful character, strong in all the spiritual qualities of the truest manhood. However, the contrary implication, that Jesus was an emotional, high-strung person, quick-tempered, going about, as the saying is, with a chip on His shoulder, and inclined in outbursts of violent temper and heated passion to resort to strong arm tactics on those who crossed His path, is equally untrue.

From the simple reading of the Gospel narratives the main impression one gets is that Jesus was a gentle, well-poised personality, strong and positive in character, kind to the unfortunate, loving toward all men, forgiving and redemptive toward the sinner. His character attracted children and women especially because He was strong and kindly and they felt sure they could count on His help and blessing. How many times do we read that Jesus was moved with compassion for needy and afflicted persons! This was surely a mark of spiritual strength and not of weakness. In the scenes of His arrest, trial, and crucifixion, Jesus acted in no sense weakly or ignobly. In strength of character He was far above those who were dealing with Him on that last day of His life. Jesus was strong enough and meek enough that He did not need to descend to the low level of His accusers and engage in verbal recrimination, threats, and bodily violence. In answer to Pilate's legitimate questions Jesus spoke respectfully as was fitting, but the only suitable answer to the bitter jealousy, hatred, and angry passions expressed by others was a dignified and nonresistant silence. In the crucifixion Jesus prayed for the forgiveness of His enemies and executioners, something which only a person of strong and positive character could do.

Jesus once said, "I am meek and lowly of heart" (Matt. 11:29), and His whole life corresponded with this statement. Meekness in the Scriptures is essentially a mark of strength and character. It is only the weak and those who feel inferior who resort to carnal force and violence; it is only those who have no adequate spiritual resources who use physical force. It is true that Jesus could also be stern on occasions. Sham and hypocrisy in religious profession invariably called forth His denunciations, yet these denunciations were not prompted by passion or fits of violent temper. They were not carnal attacks, but rather they were stern warnings prompted by divine love and in keeping with Christ's nonresistant character as portrayed throughout the Gospels.

The keynote to the character and the ministry of Jesus was expressed in the words of the heavenly choir to the shepherds on the night of His birth in the flesh: "Glory to God in the highest, and on earth peace among men in whom he is well pleased" (Luke 2:14). In His own words Jesus came to seek and to save the lost ones. It was not His object to attack social and political evils and to set men right through the use of force and violence. The traditional view of Christ's character as derived from the Gospels is correct rather than the view of those who would make Him out to be a potential militarist, accomplishing his ends by force.

6. WHAT IS THE CHARACTER OF CHRIST AS PORTRAYED IN THE PROPHECIES OF THE OLD TESTAMENT?

The character of Christ as revealed in the simple reading of the Gospels is confirmed by many of the prophecies concerning His coming. He is designated as the Prince of Peace (Isa. 9:7), an expression which means in the original Hebrew that the Messiah to come would be a peaceful prince or ruler. His meekness and nonresistance, such as is pictured in the Gospels, were also foretold by the prophets. The picture of the Suffering Servant in Isaiah 52:13 to 53:9 is well known and fits in perfectly with the New Testament record of its fulfillment.

The kindness and gentleness of Christ were portrayed in Isaiah 42:1-4, and Matthew noted its particular application to Jesus in His ministry, "Behold my servant whom I have chosen; my beloved in whom my soul is well pleased; I will put my Spirit upon him, and he shall declare judgment to the Gentiles. He shall not strive, nor cry aloud; neither shall anyone hear his voice in the streets. A bruised reed shall he not break, and smoking flax

17

shall he not quench, till he send forth judgment unto victory. And in his name shall the Gentiles hope" (Matt. 12:17-21).

The peaceful character of Christ was also described by the prophet Zechariah: "Rejoice greatly, O daughter of Zion; shout, O daughter of Jerusalem; behold thy king cometh unto thee; he is just and having salvation; lowly and riding upon an ass, even upon a colt the foal of an ass" (Zech. 9:9; Matt. 21:5).

It is clear that these are prophecies which describe the character of the coming Messiah in a way that is identical with the character of Jesus as He is found described in the New Testament, that is, as a peaceful, lowly character, yet withal one of moral strength and spiritual power.

7. DID JESUS, BY BEING NONRESISTANT, BECOME A WEAK PERSON WHO SUPINELY YIELDED TO SUPERIOR FORCE?

Some say that by interpreting Jesus as a nonresistant character, we make Him out to have been a feeble, weak, and unattractive kind of person.

As has been brought out under Question 6 above, Jesus, as He is portrayed for us in the Gospels, is in no sense a weak or helpless person. Of course, in the eyes of unregenerate men of the world the strong man is the one who stands up for his rights, who resents injury and insult, who strikes back when he is assaulted. The world ordinarily despises as weak and unmanly the person who suffers injury and wrong rather than to retaliate in kind, who does not resist carnal aggression, and who returns good for evil received. But the world's viewpoint is not the viewpoint of Christ.

It is clear that Jesus did not refrain from resisting evil men by the use of force because He was helpless and could not have used such means if He had chosen to do so. When Peter started to defend his Master in Gethsemane, Jesus stopped him and gave him to understand that if such resistance were in order at all, He could at the moment summon as many as twelve legions of angels to His defense. The fact is that Jesus considered carnal or physical defense on the part of His followers to be wrong, and deliberately chose to suffer death rather than to resort to its use. Through His death Christ conquered the world (John 16:33) and triumphed over all the designs of His enemies (Acts 2:36). Certainly Christ in practicing nonresistance was not a weak and helpless person. Rather did He prove thereby that spiritual strength and the power of God are far superior to carnal and worldly force for meeting the aggressions of evil men.

18

8. WHY IS JESUS IN SOME SCRIPTURES PORTRAYED AS A WARRIOR?

The statement is made by some that since the Bible in places portrays Christ as a conquering warrior, it is incorrect to think of Him as essentially a nonresistant person. And from this ground they would claim that participation in a just war for a good cause cannot be wrong for a Christian. Christians, they say, should be willing to fight in a war against evil and unrighteousness as Christ is pictured in some Scriptures as doing.

There are passages in the Scriptures where Christ is referred to as a warrior or a leader of armies against His enemies. Revelation 19:11-16 may be cited as a well-known example. Numerous prophecies of the Old Testament also speak of the Messiah as a king triumphing over God's foes and delivering His people from their enemies.

Some understand these particular references to Christ as applying to the time of His second coming, when He will come to judge the world, or according to some to rule the world, in righteousness. His judgment on Satan and the hosts of evil angels and men is accordingly pictured under the figure of a triumphant warrior. Even if this be true, it is not therefore right to infer that the prerogatives of Deity in Divine judgment are to be transferred to Christians now, before the second coming. In fact the New Testament specifically prohibits this: "Vengeance is mine, I will repay saith the Lord," hence "Avenge not yourselves" (Romans 12:19).

It is also possible, as some understand them, that these prophecies and descriptions are used as symbolical pictures of the victories which Christ is winning through the preaching of the Gospel and the salvation of souls. The picture in Revelation 19:11-16, they feel, scarcely describes a carnal conflict, for the only weapon of destruction mentioned there is the sharp sword that comes from the mouth of Christ (Rev. 19:15). Christ through the Gospel of His spoken and written word continues to make war upon the forces of evil and He wins many victories through the salvation of souls. If this be true, no endorsement of war or physical violence can be derived from this passage.

Whatever may be the exact and full meaning of those Scriptures which describe Christ as a conquering warrior, we would come back to the rule stated in Question 4 above, which is, that the follower of Christ will hold fast to that picture of Christ's character which he gets most clearly from reading the Gospels of the New Testament. This picture is fundamental for him. The time when Christ was incarnate among men was the time when

He came nearest to mankind, the time when He came most fully within the range of human observation. If His spirit and character cannot be known from this source, then we would have to conclude that we have no certain criterion for knowing what Christ is like. The simple believer will not allow his fundamental gospel picture of Christ to be blurred or cancelled out by other passages which on the surface appear to portray for Him a character of opposite qualities. He knows that Jesus Christ is the eternal Son of God, the unchanging Christ, the same yesterday, today, and forever (Heb. 13:8).

As has been noted before, there is a stern aspect of the character of Christ which is not inconsistent with His nonresistant nature as depicted in the Gospels. His work as the judge of all men may well be referred to under the figure of a warrior and the like, but this does not mean that He will accomplish His purposes by carnal force.

The fact is, a fierce conflict has been raging between Christ and the evil empire of Satan (Eph. 6:12) ever since He came to earth. Christ is the Head of the church, the leader of the forces that are attacking Satan's empire, and it is quite natural that the language of the Scriptures should picture vividly for us this conflict under the figure of battle and warfare. But this is not a warfare against flesh and blood, nor are carnal weapons used in this conflict. It is a spiritual warfare waged with spiritual weapons and spiritual armor (Eph. 6:10-18; II Cor. 10:3-5). It is a warfare which will end in total victory.

But there is no ground for identifying the wars between nations of this world with the warfare which Christ wages against Satan, even though some might wish to do so. In any case the Christian's conflict is with different weapons, and the fact that Christ is waging war against Satan affords no ground for asserting that the Christian may engage in carnal warfare.

Nor can the final judgment by God through Christ, in which all men shall be judged and the unrighteous cast into the lake of fire, be taken as a ground for Christians to take the life of unrighteous men here and now. God, the author of life, alone has the right to take it, and he alone has the wisdom to pass judgment on the true character of men. God, the perfect one, has the right to judge and to take vengeance. "Is God unrighteous who taketh vengeance? . . God forbid: for then how shall God judge the world." (Romans 3:5, 6, A.V.). Nonresistant Christians do not deny God the right to execute wrath when they insist that Christians do not have this right, and are forbidden to take vengeance.

20

9. How did Jesus win His victory over the world?

Jesus won His victory by suffering, by going the way of the cross. As we have noted, He did not resist those who hated Him and sought to put Him to death, but He was nevertheless stronger than they. The world might call Christ's life a failure, a weak life that ended in defeat and shame, but every Christian knows that His life was not a failure, it did not end in defeat. The resurrection from the dead is the proof that it ended in glorious triumph, and every new-born believer is a continuing confirmation of that eternal victory. What seemed to men as bitter defeat was God's way to the greatest victory of all. As followers of Christ we must follow in His steps. It may lead us in the way of suffering, it may be the way the world despises and scorns as failure and disgrace; but we must have a faith in Christ that makes us able to see beyond this world's horizon. Our Lord's command is: "If any man would come after me, let him deny himself, and take up his cross, and follow me" (Matt. 16:24).

10. What was Jesus' attitude toward the Old Testament Scriptures?

Many Bible teachers who write against the nonresistant faith claim that because God's people of the Old Testament waged wars it must therefore be right and necessary at times for Christians to fight in defense of their country and against the enemies of God and of the church in this age. This particular claim will be answered more fully further on. At this point, however, it is well to consider the relation and attitude of Christ to the Old Testament Scriptures.

Christ regarded the Old Testament Scriptures as the Word of God. He acknowledged them as such and urged people to search them for the proof of His own claims to be the Messiah (John 5:39). The law, He said, cannot fail to be fulfilled, no jot or tittle will prove unreliable (Matt. 5:18). At the same time Jesus let it be understood that the rules of conduct laid down and the practices described in the Old Testament were not all up to the high standard which God requires. Concerning some points He said: "Ye have heard that it was said to them of old time," and followed with, "But I say unto you," and thereby set forth the application of the commandment, principle, or rule which is to be observed among His followers. In some instances Jesus merely revealed what was the true inward intent of a commandment of the old law, as in the case of the sixth and the seventh command-

21

ments; he went behind the bare letter of the commandment to its real inner spirit and intent in the mind of God. In other instances He abolished the old rule and instituted a new principle, as for example in the matter of oath-swearing and of retaliation (Matt. 5:21-48). In the question of divorce and polygamy likewise Jesus did not sanction the Old Testament precedents but pointed men back to the original institution and purposes of marriage as first established by the Creator (Matt. 19:7-9).

From these considerations we arrive at the conclusion again that Christ is the supreme authority for the Christian's faith and practice. He is the Lord of the Old Testament Scriptures. He has given His followers new and higher standards of life. We dare not, by reference to the Old Testament standards of life, modify and adapt the principles which He taught. To do so is to desert Him and deny His lordship. When Christ sets new standards which supersede the Old Testament, we follow Christ, for we are living in the new dispensation of the Gospel, not in the old dispensation of law.

11. How did Jesus fulfill the law?

Jesus in speaking of the Old Testament law said, "Think not that I came to destroy the law or the prophets; I came not to destroy, but to fulfill" (Matt. 5:17). Christ fulfilled the law and the prophets by revealing the full will of God to men. The Old Testament was only a partial and imperfect revelation, for Christ revealed the perfect standard for faith and conduct. The Old Testament was useful and helpful so far as it went, and for the time and purpose for which it was first given. But Christ went beyond its standards; He filled up the measure of God's revelation which was but half-filled by the Old Testament revelation. Jesus also fulfilled the law by his whole life and work, that is, by "doing" that which the law was originally designed to do (accomplish) in God's great plan of redemption. What the law could not accomplish Christ did accomplish through grace, and thus fulfilled it.

12. Are Jesus' teachings on nonresistance in Matthew 5 limited to personal relations?

Sometimes it is claimed that Christ's teachings in Matthew 5 on refraining from retaliation and on returning good for evil are applicable to the personal relations of Christians among themselves, and may be practiced within reasonable limits, but are not applicable or practicable in the larger relations of community, state, and world.

The Lord Jesus, however, gave no hint or suggestion that Christians should practice these principles at some times and at other times not. Neither is it acceptable to teach that in personal relationships the Christian is required to practice these principles, but that as a citizen of the state he need not apply them, and should go to war at the nation's command and fight. All one can say to such counsels of compromise is that there is no ground or proof in the text itself for taking such liberties in interpreting the teachings of Jesus in this connection. If every person were at liberty to accommodate the teachings of Christ to his own convenience and what he considers practicable, or at the command of the State or any other secular institution, then indeed there could be no way to know with certainty how to follow Christ.

13. Did Jesus teach anything about war?

Sometimes it is said that Jesus taught nothing about war at all, and therefore we are free to engage in war. It is true that only a few times did He definitely mention war in His teachings as recorded. Once in an illustration or parable He mentioned it (Luke 14:31). Here He was illustrating the importance of counting in advance what it will cost one in self-denial in order to follow Him. He used the illustration of one ruler going out to meet another in war but first calculating carefully his chances for victory before they meet in conflict. This passage has nothing to teach us as to the rightness or the wrongness of war as such. It is simply a natural illustration used to impress upon His hearers the importance of preparing one's mind and thoughts for following Christ in self-denial in the way of the cross.

The other passage where Christ speaks of war is in Matthew 24:6: "And ye shall hear of wars and rumors of wars; see that ye be not troubled, for these things must needs come to pass; but the end is not yet." Here too no suggestion is made or implied as to whether wars are right or wrong. Jesus simply foretells their continuance in the future. In fact, His language assumes that these wars are altogether outside the personal experience of the Christians: they merely hear of them. He gives directions for their behaviour in view of the alarming reports they will hear, and gives no directions at all for their conduct as participants in the wars themselves.

Some point to the fact that Christ stated wars would continue, as evidence that He assumed His followers would naturally take part in them. There is no hint given that He assumed any such thing, but rather the opposite. In the same connection Christ foretells the appearance of false prophets, the continuance of hatred and iniquity (Matt. 24:6-12) ; yet no one would reason that He meant to suggest that His followers should abet false prophets and take part in hating and betraying others. No more did He suggest that His followers would naturally participate in the inevitable wars that occur in a sinful world.

Our conclusion must be that Jesus never discussed war theoretically, just as he never discussed any social institution theoretically, not even the church or the school. But to insist therefore that Jesus uttered no principles that apply to war is just as absurd as to insist that he uttered no principles that apply to the church or school.

14. WHAT DID JESUS TEACH ON NONRESISTANCE?

The plain and direct teaching which Jesus gave on the subject of nonresistance is found briefly stated in Matthew 5 and Luke 6. His own example and practice on numerous recorded occasions fit in well with what He taught. He taught that to be angry with a brother is equivalent to murder (Matthew 5:21-22) ; that nothing is more important in personal relations than peaceful reconciliation (Matthew 5:23-26) ; that acts of aggression are not to be returned but acts of good will instead are to be done toward the aggressor (Matthew 5:38-42) ; that Christians must love their enemies and pray for those who persecute them (Matthew 5:43-48). Christ practiced His own teachings on good-will, forgiveness, and nonresistance.

Some teach that the only reason Jesus did not use force to defend Himself and to prevent His arrest, nor allowed His disciples to defend Him, was because He had to die on the cross for the sins of the world. The implication in this is that His nonresistant attitude in that connection did not express His real person and character, but it was rather a pose which He assumed to reach a certain end.

The sufficient answer to this is that Jesus was not an actor doing things for effect. Nor was His death in any respect like that of a suicide. He could in fact have gotten Himself crucified in any one of a number of different ways. One way might have been by letting Himself be crowned an earthly king by the patriotic Jews and attempting to establish Himself as a Jewish ruler. Under such circumstances the Roman government would promptly have crucified Him. No, Jesus was nonresistant in a sincere and straightforward manner both in His teaching and in His practice. He spent His earthly life in witnessing to the truth, as He told Pilate, both by word and by deed (John 18:37). He did the whole will of God perfectly, and for this men hated and crucified Him. For this He gave His life as a ransom for many.

15. IS THE SERMON ON THE MOUNT INTENDED FOR THE CHRISTIAN TODAY?

The answer is, Yes, it is. There is no whit of contrary indication.

There are some earnest Bible teachers who admit that Jesus meant the teachings contained in the Sermon on the Mount for the members of the kingdom which He came to establish. But they teach further that, because the Jewish nation failed to accept Him as their king, He had to postpone the establishment of His kingdom until some future time. Hence they infer that the principles of living as given in the Sermon on the Mount do not really apply to the present age but will serve in some later kingdom.

But there is no evidence in the Gospels themselves that Christ did not establish His kingdom just as He purposed to do. When He first began to preach He announced that the kingdom of God was at hand, or was in existence (Mark 1:15), and at no later time did He say it was postponed. Later on He sent out the twelve apostles to preach the kingdom of God (Luke 9:2). Further along in His ministry He spoke thus of His kingdom: "The law and the prophets were until John: since that time the gospel of the kingdom of God is preached and every man entereth violently into it" (Luke 16:16). He also told the people late in His ministry that the kingdom of God is not something external, but that it was within them, or in their midst (Luke 17:21). In the very last days of His earthly life Jesus still spoke of His kingdom as being in existence. There are parables of the kingdom in chapters 20, 22, 25 of Matthew. Before Pilate Christ spoke of His kingdom as being then in existence; "My kingdom is not of this world" (John 18:36).

The simple and sincere reading of the Gospels reveals no ground for believing otherwise than that Jesus meant His teachings in the Sermon on the Mount to be the standard for the faith and practice of His followers. The teachings on nonresistance were certainly meant for practice in a world where there are evil men. What point would there be in having given such teachings for practice in some indefinite future society where all were Christians? What need or occasion would there be at all for one to pray for enemies and to show good will toward aggressors, if there

25

were none anywhere about? No, Jesus was not so impractical as that. He gave practical directions on the right way to live in this world side by side with evil men who will at times wrong others. The Sermon on the Mount is clearly for today, and the principle of nonresistance is intended as the Christian way of life in a world that is full of evil.

Those who hold that the Sermon on the Mount is limited in application to a perfect millennial age must be able to explain how and why in such an age the "children of the Father" must meet: persecution (Matt. 5:10-12), adversaries, criminal courts, judges, prisons (5:23-26), divorce and fornication (5:32), hypocrisy (6:1-18), thieves (6:19), dogs and swine (7:6), false prophets (7:15), demon possession (7:22).

16. IS IT POSSIBLE TO LIVE HERE AND NOW ACCORDING TO THE TEACHINGS OF JESUS IN THE SERMON ON THE MOUNT?

It is not possible except for those who are born again and who are willing to follow Christ and bear their cross after Him. But for those who are willing to suffer with Christ in taking His way of life it is possible to live the nonresistant life.

Some would say that the literal practice of nonresistance is absurd, for it would expose the individual and his loved ones to the wanton and malicious assault of criminals, outlaws, and gangsters. Especially, so some will say, it is unethical to refuse to resist criminals who attack helpless women and children.

It is easily possible to imagine extreme situations of a kind. But apparently the persons who delight in portraying such imaginary situations speak as if they placed no faith at all in the power of prayer, or in the power of a godly life, or in the spiritual power of a life consistently devoted to well doing and sacrificial living.

There are numerous cases on record where the lives of Christian missionaries and other persons have been saved miraculously from bandits and desperadoes through the humble practice of nonresistance. Other cases are on record where thieves and enemies were won as friends through sincere well doing in the spirit of nonresistance. Of course, not all who live nonresistantly are so saved. Some die by violence or suffer losses. But then we must remember that not everyone who tries to defend himself by force succeeds in saving his life. Some die in the struggle.

Nonresistance is something more than an isolated ethical practice, or a method for meeting single acts of aggression. It cannot exist in a selfish and unconsecrated life. It can only work in a life that is devoted to Christ in its entirety, that is imbued with the spirit of Christ, and that like Christ gives itself to others in unselfish service, sacrificial well doing, and overflowing love.

The person who has little earthly wealth, and spends a minimum for his own enjoyment, is not so likely to attract thieves and robbers as is the selfish man of wealth and pride. The man who is known to be one who devotes himself unselfishly to the doing of good to others is not so likely to have enemies and be assaulted physically as the selfish, opinionated man. And so it is the case that one must live in the spirit of Jesus Christ in all respects if he wishes to be truly nonresistant in faith and practice.

This seems like a high and challenging ideal, and it is. All Christians who conscientiously try to follow Christ are painfully conscious of how far short they come of completely following Him in thought, spirit, and deed. The Sermon on the Mount shames all of us. Yet we dare not go about to ease and satisfy conscience by lowering the standard which Christ has set and bringing it down to some convenient level where we can more easily meet it.

Many attempts to explain away and to minimize the nonresistant teachings of Jesus are doubtless inspired by a desire to interpret these teachings in some way that will make them seem more easily attainable. But that is the same as trying to bring Christ down to our human level of performance, which is to degrade Him from His high place of authority. Instead of doing that the Christian must humbly devote himself to the exacting task of following Christ to the extent of his knowledge and ability. If he falls short often in the inner spirit of the nonresistant life, that still does not say that he should give up striving to reach the high standard and shirk the bearing of the cross that is involved in so doing.

17. Did Jesus sanction self-defense?

No, not by violent means. What was said above about His teachings on nonresistance holds also in answer to this question.

We might also note a few other facts that bear on this same question of self-defense. Jesus foretold to His disciples that opposition and persecution would sometimes be their lot as they go out to do missionary work for Him. When they are persecuted they should rejoice and be glad that they can suffer for their faith in Him (Matthew 5:10-12). When they find themselves persecuted in one city, instead of defending themselves by force, they must flee to another (Matthew 10:23). When they see their country

27

about to be invaded they are to flee to the mountains and hide themselves (Matthew 24:16). Never does Jesus instruct his disciples to defend themselves by force.

Jesus never defended Himself by violent means against attempts made upon His life. At Nazareth (Luke 4:28-30) and several times at Jerusalem (John 8:59; 10:39) He escaped from hands intent upon murdering Him by slipping away and hiding Himself from His assailants. In so doing Jesus was not a coward afraid to face His enemies, nor a weakling yielding to his attackers. He simply would not descend to the low moral level on which His enemies acted, in order to resist them with the evil means which they used to attack Him.

When the Samaritans were hostile to Him and refused to allow Him lodging for the night, James and John felt it was an insult and asked whether fire might be called down from heaven to punish the hostile people. Jesus rebuked them. He told them that they had a wrong spirit in their hearts; that He came not to destroy men's lives but to save them (Luke 9:54:56).

When Peter drew his sword to defend his Master in Gethsemane, Jesus forbade him to use it, saying, "Put up again thy sword into its place: for all they that take the sword shall perish with the sword." (Mt. 26:52.) No worthier or holier occasion for self-defense or defending a friend could well be imagined, but Jesus clearly forbade it.

18. DID JESUS EVER USE PHYSICAL VIOLENCE ON PEOPLE?

Some writers claim that Jesus did not Himself practice absolute nonresistance, and that He did on at least one occasion use physical compulsion on people. As proof of this contention it is asserted that in the cleansing of the Temple, recorded in John 2:13-17, violence was used. They say that in this instance Jesus used a whip to lash the dealers in the Temple court and expel them from its sacred precincts.

This action of Jesus on the surface might appear to contradict the general picture and impression we get of Jesus' way of dealing with people from the simple reading of the Gospels. We do not believe, however, that there is here any violation of the principle of nonresistance, if the situation is correctly understood. Let us note briefly a number of points which indicate this.

First, this expulsion of the traders and their chattels from the Temple court (a large outdoor area, not a small room) was not enacted on the purely physical level, as might be superficially supposed. The proof is this: Jesus was acting alone; He had no one to assist Him; He had nothing in His hand but a whip made of cords braided together. The Temple, especially at feast season, was regularly policed by a temple guard to keep order. Even the Roman governor made it a point to spend this season in Jerusalem with a garrison of soldiers for emergency use. It is impossible to think that one lone man in a fit of anger marched in and began to lash away at a crowd, perhaps hundreds, of traders and succeeded in driving them out by purely physical force. The police guard would have speedily interfered and the men who were attacked would themselves have resisted and overpowered their lone assailant.

No, this was not a physical encounter with the persons involved. We must rather believe that Christ walked in among these people, spoke to them in a voice of divine authority, and that they, strangely awed and overcome, hastened to flee. A parallel incident would be the one in the Garden of Gethsemane, where the officers and men who came to arrest Jesus very mysteriously at first reeled backwards and fell flat to the ground (John 18:6). A similar reaction to Christ's divine authority doubtless caused the persons involved in the Temple scene to beat a hasty retreat.

The original word (*ekballein*) for "cast out" is a strong word, but it does not always signify violent expulsion. One finds it used in the New Testament of *sending* people *out* of the room where Jairus' daughter lay dead (Matt. 9:25), of the Lord of the spiritual harvest *sending forth* workers into His harvest (Matthew 9:38); of a man *taking* money *out* of his purse or pocket to pay a bill (Luke 10:35); and other similar instances. Hence no conclusive argument can be made from the word itself to prove that Jesus used physical violence in this incident.

What did Jesus do then? He used His improvised whip to drive out the animals, not the men, for that is what verse 15 really says (see Revised Version), "And he made a scourge of cords, and cast all out of the temple, both the sheep and the oxen." Nor does the text directly say that he used violence on the animals. The language certainly implies that the whip was not used on persons in any case.

Jesus drove the animals out of the Temple, tipped over the bankers' counters, and told the dove sellers to take their belongings away. No property was destroyed, for the owners could collect their animals again and set themselves up in business elsewhere. The bankers could gather up their spilled money and do likewise. The doves were not loosed by Jesus, lest they escape beyond recovery; He merely ordered their owners to take them away.

Let those who would fight because of Christ's supposed example see that they destroy no more life or property than He did here.

No, this was not a scene of violence and disorder at all. It was a miraculous display of Christ's divine authority in restoring the court of His Father's house to its rightful use and purpose. Christ did not act here in the heat of passion nor did He inflict the slightest injury on anyone in what He did.

19. HOW DID JESUS DEAL WITH MEN OF THE MILITARY PROFESSION?

Some writers point to the fact that Christ kindly ministered to a centurion and his household, warmly commended the man's unusually strong faith, and yet did not condemn the man's occupation nor ask him to abandon it. This, they say, is evidence that Jesus did not disapprove of the military profession as such.

Jesus came in contact with a centurion, or military captain, at Capernaum. This man was evidently religiously inclined and had shown his interest in the Jewish religion by erecting a synagogue for the Jews. He was probably a Gentile himself. Jesus healed a sick servant or slave of his, because, as He said, he found greater faith in this man than in anyone of Israel. In the story as told in Luke 7:1-10 nothing is said as to whether Jesus talked with him about his occupation or not. At best the argument that Jesus approved of the man's occupation is based on the silence of the narrative, and cannot therefore be conclusive.

One might grant that Jesus did not ask the man to quit his position in the army (or perhaps it was the police force). That still would not prove that military service is ever compatible with the spirit of Christ and is suitable for a follower of His. Whenever Jesus dealt with persons guilty of open personal moral transgression, He warned them to sin no more (John 5:14; 8:11). On other points not in keeping with His spirit He was content to plant the seeds of faith and love in men's hearts, believing that as they grew spiritually they would come to the full truth and make the changes required for full obedience.

This very story illustrates this method of Jesus in another respect. It was the centurion's slave whom Jesus healed. Just as there is no record that Jesus asked the man to change his occupation, so neither is there any record that He requested the centurion to set his slave (or slaves) free. Therefore one might with equal plausibility argue that it must be ethically and morally right for Christians to own human beings as slaves, and that Jesus endorsed slavery. A century ago many American clergymen would have argued this point just as positively as others now contend that a Christian may rightly fight in war because the centurion in this incident was not, so far as we know, required to resign his military commission forthwith.

By similar reasoning one could make Jesus justify many vices and crimes.

20. WHAT DID JESUS SAY ABOUT OBEDIENCE TO GOVERNMENT?

Jesus recognized established government as legitimate. The most direct answer to the above question is perhaps the saying of Christ: "Render unto Caesar the things that are Caesar's, and unto God the things that are God's" (Mark 12:17). This was His reply to the question asked of Him, whether it was lawful to give to the Roman emperor the tribute or head-tax which was levied by him. Patriotic Jews keenly resented this tax, the paying of which represented their submission to a foreign and heathen ruler. Jesus told them to pay to the emperor what belongs to him. The Jewish questioners had asked, Shall we give it to him? Jesus said, Pay it to him; it is an obligation, not a gift.

But the surprising part of Jesus' answer was, that they must also be sure to discharge in full their obligations to God. God makes demands on a person which he must meet, too. Jesus did not in this answer say precisely what the things are that belong to Caesar nor what the things are that belong to God. Regular taxes levied by governments, we may feel sure, are among the things that belong to Caesar, for that was the immediate subject of discussion here. Ordinary submission and obedience to laws would undoubtedly come under the same head.

Most opponents of nonresistance will insist strongly that military service demanded by the government must be reckoned among the things that belong to Caesar, and must therefore be given by all citizens regardless of personal convictions and preferences. Yet Jesus did not say that military service is such an obligation. The fact that He also emphasized the duty of paying one's obligations to God would clearly show that He was not sanctioning unlimited obedience to government.

The question is, can one ever take part in carrying on warfare and at the same time be paying to God the obedience which is His due, for it is a Scriptural principle that obedience to God must always have priority on the Christian's loyalty ahead of human demands. It is the conviction of nonresistant Christians that participation in war involves disobedience to God and a deviation from the standard which Christ has set up by precept and example for His followers, and it is therefore wrong. The Christian

31

has pledged himself to follow Christ all the way, to discharge his obligations to God first of all, and secondarily, in so far as he can, to be obedient to the demands of government.

Christ did not only sanction the paying of the tax levied by the Roman emperor. He also was careful to pay the regular Jewish Temple tax, the half-shekel assessed of every male Jew by the religious authorities at Jerusalem. He did this, even though technically He might have claimed exemption as God's Son from helping to pay for the up-keep of His own Father's house (Matt. 17:25-27). He did not thereby endorse and retain for His Kingdom the entire Jewish civil and religious code. Where no essential principle or right was involved, Jesus complied with the requirements of established human organizations, so as to avoid misunderstanding and unnecessary conflict. The same principle governs the attitude of the sincere follower of Christ.

21. WHAT WAS JESUS' ATTITUDE TOWARD POLITICAL ISSUES AND QUESTIONS OF THE TIME IN WHICH HE LIVED?

Christ practically ignored the political questions that agitated the people of that time. From reading the Gospels and the things Jesus said one would scarcely guess that there existed any serious political issues in His time. The question of paying the emperor's tax was just one such issue. In expressing Himself on this question Jesus refused to take a partisan attitude; His reply took a definitely religious turn. Jesus avoided entirely the low level of selfish and carnal thinking which generally characterizes political controversy.

From the Jewish historian Josephus we learn that there was in Palestine, at the time Jesus lived there, a great deal of unrest, dissatisfaction, and underground resistance to Roman rule. At different times Rome had to put down agitators and insurrection with an iron hand. Roman garrisons were kept in readiness close by practically all the time for that purpose, and the frequent mention of soldiers in the New Testament distinctly reflects that fact. The questions of the time which agitated the people most, centered round Jewish political autonomy, nationalism, independence, patriotism, and the like.

So far as the record in the Gospels goes Jesus took no notice of, and no direct interest in, these matters. His silence is quite striking when viewed against the background of the actual conditions then existing. He gave His life and His energies to the more important work of helping the needy, of releasing a more kindly spirit in the sin-weary world, of reaching the hearts of men and women and changing them. He sowed the seeds of spiritual truth, some of which sprang up and brought forth fruit in due season. He sought and saved the lost souls of men. But to the affairs of worldly politics and the issues over which men were ready to fight and die Christ was apparently quite indifferent. Christ's disciples should follow Him in this as in all other matters.

22. What was Jesus' attitude toward tyrannical rulers?

Jesus refrained from denouncing such rulers or encouraging people to hate and agitate against them. Several incidents appear in the Gospels which illustrate this nonresistant attitude on His part.

At one time some folks reported to Him the cruel deed of Pilate, the Roman governor at Jerusalem, who had executed some Galileans while they were engaged in worshiping in the Temple at Jerusalem, and that he had mingled their blood with their sacrifices. Jesus refused to comment on Pilate's part in this atrocious outrage. Instead of entering upon a denunciation, He utilized the occasion to utter a stern warning to the people, that they must repent of their sins including whatever hatred or ill will they held against their rulers, else they would all perish in the same way (Luke 13:1-3).

At another time Herod Antipas, the local ruler in Galilee, cruelly and unjustly executed John the Baptist to satisfy the spite and hatred of his illegal wife Herodias (Matt. 14:3-12). We do not read that Jesus issued any violent denunciation of Herod for his wickedness, or made any comment on the tyrannical deed of this ruler. Jesus, of course, did not sanction such atrocious deeds. He merely refused to step down to the base attitude of hating unjust rulers or inciting others to hate them or agitate against them. He wanted men to learn to see the spiritual issues of life, and to get right with God through repentance and a new life. Jesus had a better way to deal with ruthless despots than by hatred and violence.

23. Did Jesus authorize violence and killing when he told His disciples to buy swords?

It is taught by some that the fact that Jesus on one occasion advised His disciples to provide themselves with swords proves that He did not exclude all measures of self-defense for His followers.

The passage in question is found in Luke 22:35-38. At first glance this incident may appear to contradict what Jesus taught and practiced during His entire ministry. Such an open contradiction makes us wonder whether we really understand what Jesus meant to teach, whether He literally taught that His disciples should possess swords, even at the cost of going without garments, for it seems quite unreasonable that a single incident such as this should be allowed to negate and overthrow the plain meaning of scores of other things that Jesus said and did during His earthly life. We believe that this passage rightly viewed and understood does not contradict the nonresistant teaching of Christ in the Gospels.

The incident referred to occurred on one of the last days before the Lord's crucifixion. He wanted to prepare the disciples for the time when He would no longer be with them as their immediate leader and provider. When on earlier occasions He had sent them out on *short* tours for preaching and healing, they had been instructed to go without special provisions. They had done so, and now confessed that they never found themselves in want when they followed His directions.

But from henceforth, He tells them, their circumstances will be different. They will need to travel *farther* afield as His missionaries and representatives, not merely on *short* journeys. For this they must make preparations, taking provisions and equipping themselves for emergencies. Jesus must obviously have referred more to the mental and spiritual attitudes required for facing the future tasks than to the few material articles which are named in verse 36. For certainly their real and essential equipment for going out into a hostile world as His representatives was not a purse and a traveling bag and a sword! It was much more the Holy Spirit (Acts 1:4-8) and Christ's own spiritual presence (Matt. 28:20). No one would seriously contend that the few material articles named are to be the extent of the Christian's equipment for facing a hostile world in the name of Christ. The purse and wallet and sword are therefore more than likely symbolical of the preparation they must make.

This interpretation is borne out in what follows. The disciples promptly produced two swords. They had taken His words about having a sword quite literally. Jesus saw they had missed His meaning entirely and said, "It is enough," a phrase meaning, "Enough of that," or "Enough said," a phrase commonly used in dismissing a subject of discussion. He saw that they would have to learn His real meaning through experience. This they did later in Gethsemane when Peter, starting to defend His Master with one of these very swords, was rebuked and told to put up the

34

sword into its sheath. To interpret "it is enough" to mean that "two swords is enough, so do not buy twelve swords" would be to say that Jesus changed His mind about the need for each disciple having a sword for self-defense.

Incidentally the possession of weapons by the disciples at the moment of the arrest of Jesus would also lend some color to the accusation made against Him before Pilate a little later, namely, that He was a political agitator against Roman rule (Luke 23:2, 14). This fact would be a symbolical fulfillment of the statement in Isaiah 53:12; He was reckoned with the transgressors, or with the lawless criminals (Luke 21:37). The real fulfillment, of course, took place in the crucifixion, when He hung among the bandits.

It should be said further, that even if Jesus had meant that the disciples should literally equip themselves with swords, this would not mean they were to use them to slay other men in self-defense. The short dagger carried on the person might have other and more legitimate uses, such as for killing and slaughtering animals, cutting wood for fuel in emergency, and so forth.

Christian missionaries through all the centuries, who have gone forth with the Gospel of Christ among dangerous heathen and cannibal tribes, have never inferred from this passage that they must go forth fully armed in self-defense. Certainly the words of Christ to the apostles here would apply to missionaries if they applied to anyone, for He was talking about their going out to do work for Him. Nevertheless, true missionaries of the Gospel of salvation have always gone forth unarmed and defenseless. They have instinctively felt that to be equipped for defending their natural lives was inconsistent with the message they carried and disloyal to the Master they represented. Some pioneer missionaries have at times lost their lives through the violence of enemies, but in so doing they were most truly following their nonresistant Master, and their death in itself was a testimony for Christ the Saviour of men. And while God has not always seen fit to protect and spare the lives of His true followers, yet it is true that "nonresistance is its own best defense," and God's guardian angels are still a better defense than the best guns man has ever produced.

We may be sure that in speaking of "swords" here, Jesus did not revoke His words in Matthew 10:16: "Behold I send you forth as sheep in the midst of wolves; be ye therefore wise as serpents, and harmless as doves." Whether we can find a satisfactory interpretation of the Luke 22 incident or not, we will not surrender the plain teaching of Jesus' own nonresistance found elsewhere.

35

24. Why did Jesus speak some parables in His teaching which involved details of physical violence, capital punishment, war, and the like?

Some writers point out that since Jesus employed violent actions as features of some of His parables and illustrations, therefore these actions must be right for the Christian under some circumstances.

The reference is to such parables as in Luke 14:31, of the king with an army marching to meet another king with an army twice as large; in Matthew 22:7, of the king who sent his armies to destroy the people who had spurned disrespectfully the invitation to be guests at his son's wedding, and in addition had slain the messengers sent to invite them; and in some other parables.

A parable is purely an illustration and not necessarily a historic incident, and it is a recognized principle that no argument can be drawn from the details of an illustration. We cannot infer that Jesus approved of war-making, or wrathful, vindictive punishment, or cruel vengeance on the part of His followers, merely because He happened to use such details in His vivid and colorful parables. Parables are essentially word-pictures, and the artist may use details and accessories to make an impressive picture, details which may have no direct connection with the message which he means to convey in his picture as a whole. A parable always carries a lesson, a central message, when taken as a whole and in connection with its context; but the details cannot necessarily be made the basis for moral or ethical teaching.

This fact can be clearly seen in considering a few details of certain parables. In Luke 16:1-9, one of the main characters of the parable is a fellow who embezzled funds and falsified his superior's accounts. Still we would not feel free therefore to teach from this parable that it must be sometimes right to be dishonest in business and unfaithful to one's trust. Again, human slavery figures as a detail in many of Christ's parables, yet we do not think of teaching from these that it is therefore right and necessary for Christians to own slaves for that reason. In Luke 12:46 Jesus said the owner of a faithless slave shall surprise him in his wicked mischief and shall punish him by cutting him asunder, that is, flogging him to death on the spot, as was the legal right of owners and sometimes the actual experience of disobedient slaves in those days. Shall we infer then that it is right for Christians to own slaves and to exercise over them the absolute right of life and death, merely because Jesus used this detail from the customs of His day in a very vivid parable? No, nothing of the kind! Neither can any argument against nonresistance be brought from the details of parables which Jesus spoke.

25. DID NOT JESUS SAY HE CAME TO SEND A SWORD ON THE EARTH?

Jesus Himself disclaimed, according to some writers, the idea that He came to bring peace to the earth.

In Matthew 10:34 Jesus says, "Think not that I came to send peace on the earth; I came not to send peace but a sword." The word "sword" in this passage is used figuratively for personal conflict and division, as Jesus goes on to say in the next two verses.

The Christian Gospel has many times caused division in families and in communities where some persons accepted Christ and others rejected Him. This happens, not because those who accept the Christian faith become quarrelsome and belligerent toward those who do not believe the Gospel, but solely because the unbelievers oppose and persecute those who become Christians and forsake the ways of sin. Believers under such circumstances are instructed to be nonresistant and meek in spirit so as to win their opponents, if possible, to the same faith. This is taught at many places in the Scriptures; see particularly Luke 6:27-38 and I Peter 2:18-25. Such division and opposition constitute the "sword" which Jesus "sends" on the earth.

26. DID NOT JOHN THE BAPTIST ENDORSE MILITARY SERVICE BY GIVING ADVICE TO SOLDIERS?

It is claimed by some that because John the Baptist did not advise inquiring soldiers to desert the army and change their occupation, military service must be legitimate for Christians.

The soldiers who came to John for baptism asked of him what they must do in order to bring forth fruits corresponding to their repentance (Luke 3:14). John said they should not use violence to extort money or other things from people, they should not accuse people wrongfully, and they should be satisfied with the wages they get. It is true, we do not read that John said anything in the way of criticism of their occupation.

The main point to observe in connection with this incident is that John the Baptist did not belong to the Christian era. He still lived and labored in the pre-Christian era of the Law and the Prophets (Luke 16:16), and he held to the Old Testament standards in outlook and ethics rather than to the higher standards established by Christ. For this reason no guidance for the Christian on the question of soldiering can be gotten from the advice of John the Baptist to the soldiers. It is to Christ that the Christian looks as his Leader, as his Lord and King, as the supreme authority for his faith and for the way he is to live, not to John the Baptist. Christ had not yet begun His public ministry or given His teaching when John spoke to the soldiers.

27. DID THE APOSTLES OF CHRIST PRACTICE NONRESISTANCE?

Some would point to Paul's sharp reply in Acts 23:3 to the high priest Ananias, when the latter had ordered someone to slap him on the mouth, as proof that the apostle did not hold to the practice of nonresistance.

Paul was before the Sanhedrin at the time. He had just started to speak in his own defense when he was ignominiously struck on the mouth. He resented the insult and replied in no uncertain words to the high priest who had instigated the offense. Paul was of course human, and if he failed to act as Christ did under similar circumstances, that was a mistake, indeed a sin, on his part. But Paul's sin cannot be an example for us to repeat this sin after him. Nor does this incident from the apostle's life justify an attempt to disparage the principle of nonresistance as taught and practiced by Christ. Paul at another time quarrelled sharply and bitterly with Barnabas, an incident which does not stand to the credit of either of them as Christians.

At Philippi Paul and Silas were rashly and illegally beaten and flung into prison. Later when there was opportunity they modestly made known the fact that they were Roman citizens, and quietly insisted on being treated like citizens (Acts 16:35-39). In so doing they were not angry, nor did they later report the illegal conduct of the local officials to the higher authorities in order to get revenge for their mistreatment. They quietly left town as they had been requested to do.

Paul at different times made use of his Roman citizenship, nevertheless one notes that he never insisted upon his rights as such, nor did he use these rights in order to bring his enemies to judgment and punishment. His appeal to the emperor for a hearing and trial was not an attempt on Paul's part to get judgment pronounced against his enemies; rather it was his wish to gain his freedom and at the same time, if possible, obtain the emperor's sanction to preach the Gospel of Christ without molestation.

We can safely say that the apostles consistently followed in the nonresistant way of their Lord and Master. They suffered wrong and joyfully bore persecution rather than defend themselves by carnal means. The first Christian martyr Stephen is a shining example of those who had in their hearts Christ's spirit of love and forgiveness toward their persecutors. Stephen's dying prayer was that God should not lay the sin of executing him to the charge of its perpetrators, a prayer which reminds us of the Saviour's prayer at the time of His crucifixion (Acts 7:60; Luke 23:34).

28. WERE THE APOSTLES UNRESERVEDLY AND UNQUESTIONINGLY SUBMISSIVE TO GOVERNMENT?

It can be said that the apostles were obedient to the authorities of government in so far as nothing was asked of them that was contrary to the will of God. The apostles knew they were commissioned by Christ to be His witnesses in the world, and they refused to stop teaching in Christ's name at the request of the ruling officials at Jerusalem (Acts 4:19, 20; 5:29). Peter tersely expressed the principle which they followed: "We must obey God rather than men."

For a considerable time in the history of the early church, the Roman imperial government protected the Christian missionaries against Jews and others who persecuted them. Paul and Peter both counselled submission to that government in almost unqualified language (Romans 13 and I Peter 2). Later on the Roman government itself changed its attitude and became hostile to the Christian faith and persecuted its leaders and adherents. The same Paul and Peter who had earlier counselled submission to rulers, when that time came, refused to give up their faith in Christ upon the demand of the government. It was for this refusal, no doubt, that they suffered death as martyrs. The apostles were submissive to government, but not unreservedly or to the extent of denying Christ's authority. Christ stood above all other authorities for them, and so must He stand for every Christian believer still.

29. DID THE EARLY CHURCH SANCTION THE MILITARY PROFESSION?

Some say that the admission of Cornelius, a Roman military captain, into the church at Caesarea by Peter, shows that among the early Christians no conscientious scruples existed against the military profession. Peter, they claim, did not require Cornelius to change his occupation before consenting to baptize him as a member of the church.

The story of the conversion of Cornelius is told in Acts 10.

This man was of a pious turn of mind and had long been practicing features of the Jewish religion. When Peter preached to him and his household, they believed, the Holy Spirit fell upon them in power, and they were baptized as members of the Christian fellowship. The incident reminds us in some particulars of Christ's contact with the centurion at Capernaum (Luke 7:1-10), which has been discussed in Question 19 above. The same circumstance mentioned in that case has to be taken into account here. We do not know what all was said by Peter to Cornelius, especially during the several days that he stayed as a guest in the man's home. The argument that this incident is a sanction for the Christian engaging in military service again rests on the silence of the narrative, and cannot be regarded as conclusive.

Even though the Holy Spirit fell on these converts, which divine act left no doubt that they were eligible for baptism, it may still be considered doubtful whether Cornelius' subsequent growth in grace and Christian understanding could have left his conscience at ease as to his occupation. Naturally we cannot know as to that. The only argument for his continuing as a soldier is the weak argument from silence, which is one of the weakest of all arguments. After all, who can say that Cornelius did not quit his soldiering. The weight of the argument is in favor of his quitting.

The fact is that for the two and one-half or three earliest centuries of its history the Christian church testified uniformly against the military profession, and it is an established fact that Christians did not serve in the armies of the time. A very thorough study of all the available evidence on the subject was made some years ago by an English scholar, C. J. Cadoux, and his findings were published in a book entitled, *The Early Christian Attitude to War*. This exhaustive study of the evidence reveals the fact that the early Christians did not compromise on nonresistance nor did they participate in military service to any significant extent before the fourth century, that is, after Constantine gave Christianity the official support of the Empire. It was through the writings of St. Augustine that the church was finally influenced officially to sanction the right of Christians to fight in the armies. As long as the church was not a state church it was fundamentally nonresistant, but when it made the deadly compromise of state churchism it accepted the military system as well and abandoned its original nonresistant faith.

30. Must not the Christian, according to Romans 13:1-7 and I Peter 2:13-17, submit to government and render military service when he is called upon to do so?

The passage in Romans 13 is cited by many writers who oppose nonresistance as clear proof that the Christian along with other citizens must serve in wartime to defend his country. The state, they say, is ordained of God to bear the sword and thereby restrain wrongdoers. In this work all citizens of the state are required to do their equal and full part; their personal conscience must be made subservient to the demands of the state. To resist the demands of the state is in fact the same as resisting God's ordinance, so the argument runs.

The first point to note in reading Romans 13:1-7 is the fact that the powers that be, of which the apostle speaks, namely, the government and its officials, are something aside and apart from the Christians and the church. The implication of this fact clearly is that the believer himself is in no way directly connected or in any wise identified with the powers that be, the ruling government. His part is that of submission, doing that which is good, paying his obligations in the form of tribute, custom, respect, and honor. Paul viewed the institution of government objectively, as someone looking upon it from the outside. The Christians are not in "the powers that be." The church is not to be a part of the state, nor is the Christian to be an integral part of the government that bears the sword for a terror to the evildoers.

The main point the apostles Paul and Peter are teaching in these passages is that Christians must be submissive citizens, even though in this world they are only strangers and resident aliens whose true citizenship is in heaven (I Peter 2:13). They must never work against established government, and in no case seek to overthrow a government; this is what Paul meant by resisting the power (Romans 13:2), and this is what he was teaching against. He did not have in mind the point of refusing to comply with particular demands that a government might make upon the Christian. The apostles were not resisting government when they refused to stop preaching in the name of Jesus and declared they had to obey God rather than men. The fact is that later on the Roman government did make demands with which the Christians refused to comply. They were required to offer a bit of incense before a statue of the emperor as the proof of their loyalty and good citizenship. They refused to perform this simple and seemingly insignificant act of idolatrous worship, and were

41

in many instances executed for their refusal. Paul and Peter themselves met death as martyrs, evidently because they refused to give up their faith in Jesus Christ at the demand of the government.

Even the writers against nonresistance admit that there are circumstances in which Christians must refuse to obey government authorities, as in those just cited. Yet many say that military conscription is not one of these, and their reason for saying this is apparently that they are convinced on other grounds that war is legitimate for Christians. If it is ever right to refuse to do something a government demands, then it is also right to refuse to perform military service which violates the principles of the Gospel of Christ, provided it can be shown from the New Testament that this is the case, and we believe this can be done.

31. SHOULD NOT ONE DO ALL THAT A "CHRISTIAN" GOVERNMENT ASKS OF HIM?

Some would say that the early Christians refused to obey the pagan, unchristian government which then existed, when they were asked to perform idolatrous worship or to deny their faith, but under "Christian" governments of today, where the Christian faith is protected, Christians should submit and obey in all respects, including the rendering of military service.

To speak of "Christian" governments confuses the issue on this question. It is true there are governments today which tolerate the Christian faith and protect Christians in the full exercise thereof, and which act upon some Christian principles in their policies. But it is nevertheless incorrect to speak of these as "Christian" governments. The governments do not claim to follow Christ, nor do they practice His way of life; they include officials who are not Christian, even atheists. Some look upon the government of the United States as Christian. However, George Washington, who should know, being one of the original founders of this government, plainly stated that this government is not Christian. He meant to say it was a secular government, not intended to be Christian in any Scriptural sense, and aiming to be religiously neutral. And where is the government today that earnestly attempts to follow the whole counsel of God?

There is no more reason why the Christian who is conscientious to follow and obey Christ should today blindly submit to all the demands of a modern so-called Christian government than there was for the early Christians under the pagan rule of the Roman empire to do everything that was asked of them. The rule and authority of Christ must always be the standard by which the Christian judges every demand that comes from a government or its officials.

32. ARE NOT THE GOVERNMENT AND ITS OFFICIALS ORDAINED OF GOD? SHOULD NOT THE CHRISTIAN OBEY THEM AND LEAVE WITH THEM THE MORAL RESPONSIBILITY FOR WHAT IS DONE BY HIMSELF IN WARTIME?

Some writers who oppose nonresistance base their plea for complete obedience to government by the Christian on the contention that the state or government and the church are equally and divinely ordained of God. The deduction drawn from this contention is that the Christian citizen is therefore required to give equal obedience and service to the two areas represented by these respective institutions.

It is not correct to make the church and the state parallel institutions, equally divine and in the same sense ordained of God. The church is the body of Christ; it is God's spiritual temple; it is the household of faith. Government on the contrary is secular and exists on the level of sinful, unregenerated mankind, and has nothing to do with Christ. God has ordained government in the same sense as He has ordained and established all the natural and moral laws and principles in the universe, including those of astronomy, chemistry, and physics. When Paul says, "The powers that be are ordained of God" (Romans 13:1), he evidently refers to the same thing as when Peter speaks of the government as the "ordinance of men" (I Pet. 2:13).

The principle of social organization as expressed in organized government is divinely ordained, it is divinely implanted in human nature. As such it has a divinely ordained place, but yet outside the realm of grace. Christians are required to submit to government and its officials, and to refrain from all attempts to overthrow it, but they are not allowed to set government above or on an equal plane of authority with Christ and His will.

The moral responsibility for evil acts done in war cannot be disowned by the one who performs them. He cannot set aside his own conscience and commit moral responsibility to the state. As a free moral agent before God, he is accountable for what he consents to do. If this principle of personal moral responsibility is not at all times maintained, then it never holds, for anyone could secure an order from another person which would relieve him of responsibility for his own acts. For instance, since the

43

family is also ordained of God, a son could be relieved of responsibility for acts committed by order of his father.

33. IS NONRESISTANCE TAUGHT IN THE NEW TESTAMENT EPISTLES?

Yes. See Romans 12:18-21: "If it be possible, as much as in you lieth, be at peace with all men. Avenge not yourselves, beloved, but give place unto the wrath of God; for it is written, Vengeance belongeth unto me; I will recompense, saith the Lord. But if thine enemy hunger, feed him; if he thirst, give him to drink; for in so doing thou shalt heap coals of fire upon his head. Be not overcome of evil, but overcome evil with good." I Thessalonians 5:15: "See that none render unto any one evil for evil; but always follow after that which is good, one toward another, and toward all."

The positive aspect of the nonresistant faith is repeatedly taught in the Epistles. The Christian must be unceasingly aggressive in doing good, in showing patience and kindness, and in loving others (Galatians 6:10). His only defense against slander, misunderstanding, calumny, abuse, and persecution is to be unceasing in well doing and blessing to others. In the First Epistle of Peter this positive aspect of Christian nonresistance is emphasized repeatedly. See I Peter 2:12, 20; 3:9, 16; 4:1-4, 19.

The objection may be raised that while much good may be done by taking the patient, nonresistant attitude, there will always be some persons so evil in nature as not to respond to kindness and good will, and that the aggressions of these must be met by the use of force and violent opposition of some kind. The Christian answer is that the Christian way to meet such persons is to suffer for doing right, to follow Christ, and to bear the cross with Him, even unto death if need be. No other teaching is given anywhere in the New Testament.

34. WHY DO THE WRITERS OF THE EPISTLES USE MILITARY FIGURES AND MILITARY LANGUAGE SO FREELY, IF IT IS WRONG FOR THE CHRISTIAN TO ENGAGE IN ACTUAL WARFARE?

Some writers contend from the fact that in the Epistles military figures are used freely and without apology that this is proof that their writers did not regard military life and activity as incompatible with the Christian life.

The same answer in large part applies here as was given in regard to the use of details of violence and war found in some of Christ's parables. See Question 24 above.

44

Figures of speech and illustrations for spiritual truth are most naturally drawn from those areas of life and experience that are readily familiar to the people. They are taken from phases of life which naturally make a marked impression on the mind and hence make the truth which is presented most vivid and forceful.

There is, of course, a real spiritual conflict going on between truth and error, between right and wrong, between sin and righteousness, between Christ and Satan. To represent and illustrate this spiritual conflict, what is more natural than to draw some figures of speech from military life, specially in view of the fact that the Roman soldier was very much in evidence in the world of that day. See Ephesians 6:10-18; II Timothy 2:3, 4; I Timothy 1:18. Not nearly all of the apostle Paul's figures and illustrations for the Christian's spiritual conflict are drawn from military life; many are also taken from the life of the Greek athletes (II Timothy 4:7; I Corinthians 9:24-27; Philippians 3:12-14).

The use of these figures cannot be pressed to prove that the apostles meant to sanction either carnal warfare or pugilism for the Christian. If that were permissible, then Paul would also be sanctioning thievery and housebreaking for Christians, since he compares Christ's coming to a thief in the night (I Thessalonians 5:2).

35. Is THE PRESERVATION OF CHRISTIANITY DEPENDENT ON THE FORCE OF ARMS?

Some writers oppose nonresistance because they appear to believe that the present-day attacks on the church and on the Christian faith cannot possibly be met by any means other than superior military force. They mean to imply that the Christian who refuses to fight against the anti-Christian dictators is disloyal to Christ and a traitor to Christian civilization.

We must view this contention in the perspective of history. If the defense of the Christian church and the preservation of the Christian way of life were actually dependent on military force of arms, then Christianity could never have survived the first two centuries of its history. The apostles did not go about armed for self-defense, and Christian missionaries have never done so. The early church did not fight with carnal weapons in self-defense against the determined attempt of the powerful Roman empire to crush it in repeated persecutions. Instead of resisting its persecutors by force the church suffered, and the blood of the martyrs became truly the seed of the church. The suffering church

45

proved to be a growing and finally a triumphant church, while
the mighty persecuting empire fell into dust.

Those who suppose that they must fight in battle to preserve
Christianity lack trust in God and His power. Christ foretold that
even the gates of Hades shall not prevail to overthrow His church.
If Christians follow Christ in obedience and sacrifice and suffering and doing good to all men, they will be doing more to preserve the church from its enemies than if they resort to the
world's carnal means for carrying on a spiritual conflict.

36. IS THE GOD OF THE OLD TESTAMENT DIFFERENT FROM THE GOD OF THE NEW TESTAMENT?

Some say that in making the nonresistant standard of conduct
essential for the New Testament ethic we are guilty of teaching
that two different Gods are portrayed in the Bible. Since this idea
is contrary to sound theology, these teachers seek to harmonize the
ethics of the Old and New Testaments by making the O.T. standard supreme and then minimizing the nonresistant teachings of
the N.T. so as to make these subsidiary or inapplicable. By this
line of reasoning from O.T. precedents they think to justify the
Christian's participation in war in obedience to the call of his
government.

The solution which these teachers propose is not the correct
one. It is in fact just the reverse of the way the Christian must
proceed for harmonizing the ethical standards of the Old and
New Testaments. Jesus Christ is the highest authority on faith
and conduct for the Christian. He is Lord also of the Old Testament. He must really be the Lord and King of the Christian's life.
The way of life which He revealed has superseded the partial
revelation, the lower standards and precedents of the O.T. period. This is the Christian's position as a matter of faithfulness and
loyalty to his Master. The teachings of Christ on nonresistance
and good will are today the right standard. The O.T. standards of
conduct are subordinated to Christ. They must be understood and
explained in reference to Christ's teaching, instead of Christ's
teaching being explained away by reference to the Old Testament.

The fact is that the difference between the nature of God as revealed in the O.T. and in the N.T. is by some grossly misunder-
stood. It is not right to say that in the former God is primarily a
God of war and battle, or wrath and revenge, and that in the latter He is a God of love and mercy and forgiveness. In the N.T.
God's justice and His judgment on sin are brought out no less
clearly and emphatically than His love and mercy. And in the

46

O.T. again His mercy and forgiveness are even more prominently displayed than His wrath and judgment. His gentleness and patience in dealing with the wayward Israelites for many centuries are strikingly outstanding. "Jehovah, a God merciful and gracious, slow to anger, and abundant in loving-kindness and truth"—this verse and its truth run like a refrain through much of the O.T. (Ex. 34:6; Num. 14:18; Deut. 4:31; Neh. 9:17; Psa. 86:15; 103:8; 145:8). Whereas God punished sin and iniquity even unto the third and fourth generations, He at the same time promised His mercy and loving-kindness to a thousand generations of those who loved Him and kept His commandments.

That there is a marked difference between the practices of God's people in the O.T. and what is required of Christians in the N.T. is apparent to every Bible reader. The former frequently practiced polygamy, divorce, concubinage, war, retaliation, and so forth, none of which are allowed in the N.T. But it is not necessary to hold that two different Gods are responsible for this difference in the practices noted.

The O.T. records for us the beginnings of God's revelation of the plan of redemption and of His will for men. This revelation was progressive over long centuries of time through various saints and prophets. We can understand that this revelation was in every period more or less adapted to the spiritual level and the spiritual capacity of the people to whom it was given, and that this fully accounts for the differences between the standards of practice allowed in the O.T. and what has now been revealed through the incarnate Christ as the final standard of faith and practice for the Christian. This was evidently the attitude of Jesus toward the O. T. revelation.

The apparent difference is further also due to the fact that in the O.T. God was dealing with people on a different basis than He does now in Jesus Christ. There is nothing incompatible in this with the fact that the same God was revealing Himself in both Testaments. In the Old Testament God dealt with his people under the form of a theocracy governed by the law given on Sinai, whereas in the gospel dispensation God deals with His people as His children on the basis of grace through faith and obedience. "For in Christ Jesus neither circumcision (the law) availeth anything, nor uncircumcision; but faith working through love." (Gal. 5:6.) See also the whole discussion of Galatians 3 and 4.

37. WHY DID GOD COMMAND THE ISRAELITES TO DESTROY THE CANAANITES IN WAR?

Many writers point to the Lord's command to the Israelites to invade Canaan and destroy all its inhabitants as proof that war in itself cannot be sin, nor under all circumstances wrong for Christians. What God has *commanded* anyone to do, so they say, cannot in itself be unconditionally wrong, and therefore there are times and circumstances when Christians may still take part in war.

One important point to keep in mind in considering this matter is the fact that Israel was a nation among other nations. She was a different and unique nation, to be sure, a theocracy in government, and a nation that was supposed to be separated in life and worship from other nations. The very fact, however, that Israel was outwardly a nation rendered her subject to many of the same conditions which affect all nations. No such theocratic nation exists in the gospel dispensation.

It is the clear teaching of the Bible throughout, that God judges and punishes sin. Sin brings with it certain evil and necessary consequences which are the judgment of God upon that sin. Nations as such do also commit collective sins. Hence nations must also be judged and punished for their sins. One form of judgment on sinful nations, according to the Scriptures, is that other nations make war upon them and in some cases destroy them. The nation that attacks another and perhaps destroys it is indirectly serving as God's agent of judgment for the sins of the nation that is attacked. But the attacking and destroying nation is also sinning in attacking another because its own purpose and will in doing so is selfish. Its aim is not to do the will of God but to grasp the land or the goods of others and take them for itself. Hence in due time it must also suffer the judgment of God for its sin. This weary round of sin and judgment is the tragic cycle in the life of earthly nations in a sinful world.

Israel as a national entity also was drawn into this recurring cycle of sin and divine judgment. No doubt they could have kept out of it, if they had lived in full obedience to God, for one finds in the instructions first given to them for occupying the land of Canaan, that the emphasis is on the fact that God will bring them into the land, that God will drive out and destroy the inhabitants of the land, on the condition that they obey Him fully (See Ex. 23:20-31; 33:2; 34:11; Deut. 7:20-26; 31:3-6). As God had delivered them from Egypt and at the Red Sea, so He could

48

have settled them in Canaan by His miraculous power and intervention. But Israel failed in obedience. They worshiped idols, they were not faithful to God, and the result was that they slipped into the tragic cycle of sin and divine judgment in which all nations as nations are involved.

Israel had to fight for their possession of Canaan. It was part of God's judgment on them, that they had to win the land by war; and the record makes it clear that they were unable to completely conquer the land, which is also part of God's judgment upon them. In their later history they were many times oppressed by foreign tribes in judgment for their sin and had to fight for their freedom. And so the bitter cycle went on. The prophet Habakkuk was greatly perplexed by this tragic cycle of sin and judgment as it affected Israel. Why should the rapacious, heathen Chaldeans be allowed to ravage Israel, he asked. And the Lord gave him to understand the meaning of this situation. Israel was suffering God's judgment for its sins, and the Chaldeans themselves were sinning in attacking Israel, and divine judgment would in turn overtake them also. See Habakkuk, chapters 1 and 2.

It was in this sense that God commanded, or rather condemned, the Israelites to fight and by their own efforts largely destroy the Canaanites whose cup of iniquity was full and ripe for God's judgment. But this judgment of God on Israel does not set any precedent for the Christian today. There is no nation of God's people today comparable to the theocracy of Israel in the O.T. God's people are a holy and spiritual nation, above and apart from the political and geographical boundaries of earthly nations. They are citizens of a spiritual realm. No conduct of Israel as a nation can be used as a standard of conduct for the individual Christian now.

To some earnest and nonresistant Bible students the above solution to the problem of the war of the people of God in the Old Testament is not acceptable. They offer an alternative solution as follows: Only the man-made wars of the Old Testament are sin. Those wars which were commanded by God specifically cannot be considered as sin, since they were ordered by God who is the sovereign over all human life and has authority to take life as well as to give it, and we cannot challenge God in his decrees. Those who hold this view teach that New Testament saints, being separate from the state, and not being members of a theocracy, receive no orders from God to engage in war, and accordingly they, as the people of God in the new dispensation, have no responsibility for carrying on war, for there are no longer any God-commanded wars and all wars are man-made.

Neither of the above solutions permits the use of the wars of the O.T. as a justification for participation in wars by the followers of Christ.

38. Are love and nonresistance taught in the Old Testament?

The fact that one reads much in the O.T. of violence, bloodshed, war, and revenge, is apt to obscure in the reader's mind the parallel fact that love and even nonresistance were to some degree taught and practiced in the Old Testament, although by no means in the same way as in the New Testament.

Isaac in his experience with the Philistine lords lived by the standard of nonresistance toward the aggressions of evil men. His experience proved that its practice is possible and that it brings favorable results (Genesis 26). The spirit and practice of Isaac suggests in many respects the teachings and practice of Christ in the New Testament.

Solomon, in contrast to his father David, was a ruler of peace. Because he was a peaceful ruler, he was commissioned to build the first Temple for the nation of Israel, a task that was considered too sacred for the hands of David who had shed much blood in warfare. (I Chronicles 22:8.)

There are also numerous teachings in the Old Testament on the duty of loving strangers and foreigners. The Israelites were forbidden to harm or to wrong a foreigner who dwelt among them; they were to treat him as they would treat a native and to love him as themselves (Leviticus 19:33, 34). They were forbidden to take vengeance or bear a grudge against their fellow citizens; they were to love their neighbors as themselves (Leviticus 19:18). The principle of doing good in return for evil, of turning an enemy into a friend by means of kindness and helpfulness shown to him, is taught in Proverbs 25:21, 22.

However it must be remembered that in this as in other Scriptural principles, while the germ was in the Old Testament the fullness of grace and truth came by Jesus Christ. What was only latent in the Old Dispensation was fully revealed in the New Dispensation.

39. Were not Retaliation and Capital Punishment Approved in the Old Testament?

In the first place, it must be said that war and capital punishment are not the same. Capital punishment is by law and is a judicial act, while war is wholly without law and justice.

Retaliation and capital punishment were given legal recognition under the Mosaic law; see Leviticus 24:17-21; Exodus 21:12-25. Some teach from this that these are still right, and that even a Christian as an officer of government may enforce such measures, or as a soldier in the army may inflict death on an enemy of his country, without thereby doing any wrong.

So far as concerns retaliation for wrongs and injuries received, the Christian does not need to be in any doubt as to his duty. For Jesus, his own Lord and Master, has given the complete answer on this point in Matthew 5:38-42. Jesus says that instead of paying back eye for eye and tooth for tooth, we must meet the aggression with love and good will. We should try to prove to the aggressor that we love him, and are interested in his best welfare, and should suggest by our reaction to his evil deed that there are better ways to treat one's fellow beings than with violence and injustice.

Further in regard to retaliation, we need to recognize that the provisions for such redress in the Mosaic law were not intended to be carried out privately between citizens. The earlier practice, the natural reaction of human anger and hatred, was to take unlimited revenge, or at least as much revenge as one could manage to get. If a man lost a tooth in a hostile encounter, he probably felt impelled to knock out as many of his antagonist's teeth as he could get at, and so on. When a man was murdered, his relatives probably took their revenge by killing not only the murderer but as many of his family and relatives as possible.

The provisions of the Mosaic law were designed to curb the natural impulse of men inspired by violent anger to exact unlimited revenge, and to place justice and redress on a legal and limited basis, authorized by an official of the law and not exacted by the individual himself. This enactment was in itself a forward step in teaching men to regard the lives and rights of others. The gospel standard of forgiveness and good will in the place of physical retaliation was another great step of advance over the Mosaic law for teaching men to help instead of injure each other, and Christ has authorized this standard for His followers.

As for capital punishment, so far as the Christian personally is concerned it too is done away, and he can have no part in it. In so far as it was an expression of the old principle of retaliation, of tit for tat, it has been done away by the same teachings of Christ that abolished the lesser forms of retaliation mentioned above. One who seeks to live by the nonresistant principle as taught by Jesus cannot feel that he is acting in the spirit of his Master when he serves as an executioner of laws and sentences that are themselves contrary to that principle. The same applies to his participation in war. As to whether capital punishment is legitimate for civil governments, this is not a question the Christian needs to decide, seeing that he is not a part of the earthly government but is a citizen of another country.

40. **Does the fact that the Old Testament heroes of faith were also men who waged wars constitute an endorsement of war for the Christian in the gospel dispensation?**

It is pointed out by some that many of the greatest men of faith and servants of God in the Old Testament were also excellent warriors. They point to Abraham, who organized an expedition for the forcible rescue of his nephew Lot when the latter was carried off as a prisoner of war. Other heroes of faith who were also famous as warriors were Joshua, Gideon, and David. Surely if these worthies could wage wars for righteous causes, so the argument runs, the Christians today can and must do the same.

As for the later men like Joshua, Gideon, David, and others, we must repeat what was brought out above, that Israel was a theocracy and at the same time an earthly nation, and her national leaders acted in line with the needs and circumstances of a nation that was at one and the same time God's people and also a nation caught in the tragic cycle of sin and divine judgments. Their practice cannot be taken as the pattern for Christians who are under the spiritual kingship of Jesus Christ, whose kingdom is not of this world.

And again, if the practices of the Old Testament heroes in making war were a legitimate precedent for Christians to follow, then it could with equal authority be claimed that polygamy, concubinage, divorce, and personal slavery are proper practices for Christians today. These latter things have at times in the past been defended as right and lawful on the basis of the practices of the Old Testament heroes, but the laws of civilized lands no longer regard them as right and no one defends them today on the basis of the Old Testament. Yet many still defend warfare and all that goes with it on the basis of Old Testament ethics.

41. DOES THE SIXTH COMMANDMENT OF THE DECALOGUE APPLY TO WAR?

Many writers argue at considerable length in their attempt to show that the commandment, "Thou shalt not kill," really means, "You must do no murder." Hence they claim this commandment cannot be used as a prohibition of all killing, but only of private and deliberate homicide. They assert that the judicial taking of life and the killing of people incident to war cannot be included under the sixth commandment.

It is sometimes difficult to follow the discussion of this labored distinction between mere killing and murder. There is, of course, a legal distinction to be made between the two. The moral distinction between them is not so clear, and the distinction ceases to exist when the man killed is considered.

The ten commandments were given as God's fundamental moral code, a high standard that expressed God's will for man's conduct. In actual practice God made some adaptations and concessions for the Israelites in forming the legal code for use under the circumstances of that time. Thus we find capital punishment specified for a series of crimes ranging from manslaughter down to the owning of a dangerous ox (Exodus 21). But these adaptations do not necessarily annul the divine intent of the sixth commandment, that men should respect the life of their fellow man and not deprive him of it. A parallel case of adaptation would be that of the Mosaic civil code on divorce. (Deut. 24:1-4). Jesus says specifically that this was an adaptation to the hardness of men's hearts in that age, but that it was contrary to God's basic will. (Mt. 19:8.) For the follower of Christ in the gospel dispensation God has made no such adaptation or concession, neither in regard to divorce nor in regard to killing.

Furthermore Jesus laid bare the real inner meaning, intent, and spirit of the sixth commandment in Matthew 5:21-26. He says that anger, ill will, and disharmony of any kind between fellow men are in fact violations of this commandment. Some theorists are quite sure that a soldier can go into battle with love in his heart for the enemy that is arrayed against him, that he may even destroy the men on the other side from the motive of love for them. But military officers do not agree to this doctrine. They do not want many such soldiers in their armies, if there actually are any such. Military leaders assert that they need men who are

53

thoroughly aroused to hate the enemy, and that men who do not hate vigorously are not good fighters.

The apostle John, who was deeply imbued with the spirit of his divine Master, taught that the person who hates his brother is in fact a murderer (I John 3:15). It is clear then that according to Christ and the apostle, every unsocial attitude toward a fellow man, whether ill will, anger, hatred, or whatever, is a violation of the divine intention expressed in the sixth commandment. It is hard to see how those who engage in the destruction of life in connection with warfare can be free from murder as Jesus defined it.

It is the contention of some that the soldier who kills in war is not acting as an individual but as a representative of his government, and that therefore he is not personally guilty of killing or of murder. But it is more than doubtful whether the individual can abdicate his moral responsibility and assign it to a government or to anyone else. The Christian knows full well that no one but himself can exercise the faith that leads to the forgiveness of his sins and to his salvation from sin. His salvation is certainly a personal matter between himself and God. How is it any more possible that the responsibility for his life and conduct can be delegated to someone else? No, the Bible does not teach us that the individual person can resign conscience into the custody of another, or that he can excuse his disobedience to Christ by pleading that a government has assumed the moral responsibility for his actions. Those who assert the contrary fail to produce evidence from the Scriptures. It might also be remembered that recognition for valor in war is granted to individuals who then wear individually the medals conferred by a grateful government. The same individual is as much personally responsible for the lives he has killed as for the heroism he has displayed.

James Russell Lowell's satire on the attitude of the man who would sell his conscience to the state concludes thus:

> "Ef you should take a sword an' dror it,
> An' go stick a feller thru,
> Guv'ment aint to answer for it—
> God'll send the bill to you."

42. DOES GENESIS 9:6 APPLY TO WAR?

Genesis 9:6 reads: "Whoso sheddeth man's blood, by man shall his blood be shed; for in the image of God made he him." It is claimed by some that this verse is the divine authorization for human government, the divine sanction for its judicial functions, including capital punishment, and the sanction for waging war. Thereby, we are told, the duty of exacting life for life is laid upon governments for all time. Along with this teaching the inference is drawn that governments are responsible to execute murderers and to wage whatever wars they may deem necessary, and further that all citizens, including Christians, are obligated to serve their government in every way it may demand of them for carrying out these functions.

This interpretation is one possible way to understand the verse, but it is not the only possible interpretation. Others understand the verse as a statement of fact, meant to serve as a warning against murder and revenge, and not as a command at all. Before the flood the earth was filled with violence and now God warns Noah that this violence will return if once again men begin to take human life.

Whatever the true interpretation may be, this passage again is not pertinent to the faith and practice of the Christian who belongs to Christ and His spiritual kingdom. The nonresistant Christian does not participate in the judicial functions of government for the reason that the duties involved in doing so frequently conflict with the spirit and tenor of Christ's teachings. Jesus was generally indifferent to the political affairs of His day. He also refused to act as arbiter of a dispute between equally selfish brothers over an estate.

Nor can it be truthfully said that every person who is employed by a modern government under license or under civil service is an integral part of that government. Government today covers a wide range of activities, and in any activity where the duties involved do not conflict with the teachings of Christ, there the Christian can serve his community and fellow men. Carrying mail and teaching school, for instance, are not parallel with serving in the armed forces. Only when such government servants are required to support war does the question of nonresistance become involved.

43. IS WAR GLORIFIED IN THE OLD TESTAMENT AS BEING IDEAL?

No, it is not. Its practice is simply recorded as part and parcel of the whole system of sin and iniquity that followed the fall of man. Several lines of evidence show that warfare and strife were not idealized in the Old Testament. One striking evidence is the fact that King David was not permitted by the Lord to build the first temple as the house of the Lord in Jerusalem. David was eminently a man of God, a man after God's own heart, a man who

55

knew God perhaps as no other person of his time and who honored God in many psalms of praise and worship; he did a great work for God's people. He conceived the idea of a temple, and he longed and planned to build such a house for the worship of the Lord.

But the Lord did not allow David the privilege of building it. The reason given was, because David had shed much blood as a warrior and had made many wars. In view of the spiritual significance of the temple for the nation, David as a warrior was not the fitting person to build this temple (I Chr. 22:8; 28:3). That work was delegated to his son Solomon, who, though a much weaker king in many respects, was nevertheless a man of peace who ruled in an age of peace. For that reason he was considered a more fitting person to carry through a work of great religious significance. The warrior side of David's life did not make him a hero in God's eyes.

Another line of evidence that war was not glorified as the ideal state of things among men even in the Old Testament is found in the fact that when the prophets saw their visions of the coming Messiah's kingdom, the ideal age of the future, they spoke of it as a time when wars shall cease and when the implements of war shall be transformed into the implements of husbandry and peaceful industry (Isaiah 2; Micah 4; Isaiah 32).

44. How shall the Christian regard the Old Testament in relation to the question of war?

Many of the writers and teachers who argue against non-resistance begin their discussion with the Old Testament, or at least base it largely on the precedents and practices recorded in the Old Testament. They appear to take the pattern for their way of thinking about war directly from this older portion of the Bible. The specific teachings of Christ are as a rule passed over lightly by them, or are explained away somehow so as to bring them into harmony with the pattern of thought derived from the Old Testament.

As has been repeatedly brought out under previous Questions, the Christian, the one who honors Christ and acknowledges the rightful authority that is His in determining the faith and life of His followers, must begin first with the teachings and the practice of Jesus Christ Himself in order to find the right position and attitude toward war. The outline and the pattern of his thinking about war must be received from Christ and not from the Old Testament.

Yet in emphasizing this we do not cast reflection on the Scriptures of the Old Testament. They are the inspired and accurate record of God's dealings with the people of early times. They reveal the important beginnings of God's program of human redemption. The very fact that they are a record of what God did fills the Old Testament with important moral and religious lessons that can be studied with profit today. As the apostle Paul wrote, the inspired Scriptures of the O.T. are profitable for teaching, for reproof, for correction, for instruction which is in righteousness (II Timothy 3:16). Considered in this way from the historical standpoint, there is nothing in the Old Testament that contradicts the principles taught and practiced by Christ; but their true place is always subordinate to Christ, and not above Him in authority.

45. Is CONSCIENCE A RELIABLE GUIDE IN REGARD TO THE QUESTION OF PARTICIPATION IN WAR?

Conscience in itself alone is not to be considered an authority on the right or wrong of any line of conduct. Conscience is only the inward monitor which tells the individual to do what he knows to be right and which condemns him for doing what he knows to be wrong. The knowledge of what is right and what is wrong must be gotten from some source outside oneself.

In the case of the Christian believer, the authority for what is right and what is wrong is the will of God, as revealed through Jesus Christ and in the Scriptures. The Christian has pledged himself to accept and follow Christ as Lord, and his conscience holds him to what he has promised to God. To violate that pledge of commitment is to compromise the integrity of his character. Such violation leads to a seared and a defiled conscience.

When some writers assert that the individual conscience is not to be considered a safe guide to follow in regard to the question of fighting in war, what they frequently mean to imply is that the conscientious objector is ignorant and misguided in his understanding of the Scriptures. His only answer is that as a Christian he knows no other course to take than to accept Christ's authority and His teachings on the principle of not resisting those that are evil.

Others admit the correctness of the C.O. position as to the meaning of Christ's teaching, but nevertheless suggest that there are times and circumstances when the individual Christian should set aside his conscience and turn over to the state the responsibility for what he does or has to do as a soldier. This the Christian

57

cannot do. His commitment to follow Jesus Christ cannot be put
into cold storage while he proceeds to engage in what he knows
to be wrong. The believer's personality is a unity. It cannot be
divided into two compartments, in one of which he lives for Christ
when he readily can, and in the other of which he lives for the
state or some other cause when he feels he must. "No man can
serve two masters" (Mt. 6:24), says Jesus.

46. Do NONRESISTANT PEOPLE REFRAIN FROM TAKING PART IN WAR MERELY IN ORDER TO SPARE PHYSICAL LIFE?

It is claimed by some who oppose nonresistance, that objectors
to war place an undue emphasis on the value and sacredness and
inviolability of human life, as though there were nothing in the
world more important than saving and sparing life.

Only God can give life and only He has the ultimate right to
bring a life to a close. A man can repent and make restitution
for many of the wrongs he may have done in his lifetime, but he
can never restore a life which he has destroyed. God extends
grace to a soul as long as a man lives, and He offers him the
opportunity to repent, believe, and be saved from sin. To cut a
human soul off from his allotted time of grace is an act too
serious for a fellow man to assume, and the more so because God
has forbidden men to kill each other.

The Christian, while he refuses to deprive a fellow man of his
life, is ready at all times to sacrifice himself and to give up his
life, if need be, in helping others, in doing good, in saving other
lives, or in witnessing for Christ to the world. He is commanded
by Christ Himself to be ready to give up his own life whenever
necessary, but he is never commanded to destroy another person's
life. For this he has the authority of Christ Himself. Christ came
not to destroy men's lives but to save them. Christ gave up His
own life in bearing witness to the truth and in doing the whole
will of God. There are some things of more value than life, and
the Christian has the right to sacrifice his own life for greater
values, but he never has the right to destroy the life of another.

47. ARE NONRESISTANT PEOPLE PARASITES ON SOCIETY, WHO RE-TURN NOTHING FOR WHAT SOCIETY GIVES THEM?

Some writers accuse the conscientious objectors to war of being
parasites on society. They accuse them of freely enjoying liberties and privileges for the winning and defending of which they
refuse to fight. They look upon them as leeches on the nation in

58

which they live, benefiting from the results of wars which others fight, but themselves contributing nothing to their country's defense.

We affirm that it is a misconception of the facts to hold that freedom and liberty are historically the products exclusively or mainly of wars and battles. War and conflict are frequently the last phases of some long process of development and education which was the instrument that gradually built up public opinion and individual conviction sufficient to support liberty. Freedom of religion and freedom of worship have historically been established through the long continued teaching and preaching of the Word of God. The martyrs who died for first advocating and practicing these principles, as for instance among the early Anabaptists, Huguenots, and other dissenters, did at least as much, and we believe much more, for the establishment of these very freedoms than the soldiers who later died on fields of battle. War has more often destroyed liberty than achieved it.

We believe also that, whatever may be the immediate crisis in which a nation happens to be, the constructive processes of peaceful society are of fundamental importance for the national welfare. Such activities as spreading the Gospel of Christ, teaching religion and morals to the young, exemplifying the spirit of Jesus Christ in human relationships, must be continued without interruption. Some must be willing to follow Christ in all-out commitment and devote themselves to these activities constantly, whatever the crisis of the moment may be. A nation mobilized one hundred per cent for the destruction of an external enemy would very likely find its inner foundations gone, its moral and spiritual fiber ruined, by the time the crisis is over, if it depended on military activities alone for its salvation. The world needs at all times the faith and life of those who seek to follow Jesus Christ and bear the cross after Him.

48. IS IT THE POLICE AND THE LAW COURTS THAT RENDER PROPERTY AND LIFE SECURE IN A COMMUNITY?

Some writers assert that nonresistance is not practical in a community, and that it is inconsistent to object to war service and yet regularly accept police protection, which, like war, is based on force.

It is true that the police power, as well as war between nations, requires the use of force. There is, however, an essential difference in that the police are regularly constituted by some higher authority to whom they are responsible. In war between nations there exists no higher court of appeal that can enforce justice; superior might and weight of arms is the final arbiter in the struggle.

For the nonresistant believer, to serve as a law enforcement officer whose duty involves the use of force in emergencies, is equally as objectionable as serving in the army. Here again he is not a slacker, benefiting from police protection and doing nothing constructive for the community. His real trust for protection and security lies not in the police or the sheriff but in God. The peaceful and orderly life of a community is not due nearly so much to the presence of a few policemen with guns and clubs, and the enforcement of certain laws, as it is to the spirit of well-doing and co-operation existing in the hearts of most of the citizens. If a majority or even a large minority of the citizens are lawless in spirit, the police and the laws are helpless to keep order. American history has numerous illustrations of the fact that it is virtually impossible to enforce a law against the resistance of any large portion of the population. Witness "prohibition."

The real forces that make for orderly community life are spiritual forces rather than external coercion. Those who teach God's Word, who get men's lives changed through the power of the Gospel, who teach morals and religion to the young, who maintain exemplary practices in home and personal life, these are the really constructive citizens in a community. There is always a fringe of evildoers who need the forcible restraint of officers of the law, but the officers are not the persons who in the final analysis render life and property reasonably secure in a community. God has provided the "salt of the earth" for that.

49. Is NONPARTICIPATION IN WAR ON CHRISTIAN GROUNDS OF RECENT ORIGIN?

No. From the time of earliest Christian history there have been those who conscientiously abstained from taking part in carnal warfare. The early Christians for about three centuries were practically a unit in regarding military service as unchristian and wrong. The dissenting and nonconforming groups of the Middle Ages, who were usually persecuted as heretics by the dominant Roman Catholic Church, did not participate in warfare. In the time of the Reformation the evangelical Anabaptists taught against war and the use of force on the part of those who claimed to be followers of Christ. Their successors, the Mennonites, have continued in this way for over four hundred years.

In our own country the ordained ministers of religion are regularly exempted from active military service. This practice seems to go back to the Middle Ages, when the Catholic clergy were always exempted from serving in the armies. The practice of exemption for the clergy was based on the idea that carnal warfare is too violent, brutal, and bloody work for the most spiritual rank in the church to engage in. The Catholics ranked the clergy as more spiritual and on a higher Christian plane of life than the rank and file of the membership of their church, and the feeling was that the bloody business of war-making was not compatible with the supposedly superior spirituality of those set aside for spiritual work and service.

The acknowledged Protestant view is that all the members of the church (all Christians) are on the same level in Christ, and presumably on a high spiritual level. The Christian feeling or instinct which leads to the exemption of clergymen from fighting should then logically apply to all Christians alike, for they are all priests to God according to the Scriptures. Protestant ministers who accept regular exemption should either acknowledge themselves superior to the lay Christians (the Catholic view) or they should demand exemption for lay Christians on the same basis as for themselves, or they should disclaim the right of exemption for themselves. The Christian tradition of clerical exemption through the centuries should lead them to take the second of these courses, namely, to demand exemption for all Christians, which is the position of the nonresistant Christian.

50. WHY DO NONRESISTANT CHRISTIANS PAY THE TAXES THAT ARE LEVIED BY THE GOVERNMENT?

Some writers claim that the nonresistant position of objection to war participation is an illusion, because these same objectors pay federal taxes, a very large part of which goes directly for war and for national defense purposes.

For the paying of taxes regularly levied by government we have the explicit authority and sanction of Christ Himself. When He was asked about the rightness of paying the emperor's head-tax, Jesus laid down the principle that to Caesar should be paid whatever belongs to him, whatever is his due. On that basis the paying of taxes has been assumed as a duty, not primarily because of the government's command, but principally because Christ authorized their payment. When the Christian pays his lawful taxes he is still primarily under Christ's authority rather than under the state's authority. The voluntary loaning of money to the government for war purposes is a different matter than the paying of taxes.

It is, of course, true that a large part of the taxes paid to the national government, especially in wartime, is used for military purposes. That is the government's own affair. The officials of government have on them the moral responsibility for what is done with the taxes they collect. The Christian cannot dictate how taxes shall be used nor is he responsible for what is done with them.

A Christian farmer raises food which some ungodly person may buy on the market and consume and use the strength from it for robbing a bank or beating some fellow man. A Christian teacher teaches a pupil to write a skillful hand, and this person later uses his writing skill for forging checks. Yet the criminal is himself morally responsible for what he does in such a case, and not the farmer or the teacher. The Christian fulfils his responsibility in doing what he knows is right, in following Christ and doing good to men, in seeking to win men away from their evil doing through the power of the gospel.

51. IS NONRESISTANCE THE SAME AS PACIFISM?

The terms "pacifist" and "pacifism" are in themselves legitimate words, in fact they are Scriptural terms, so far as that goes. Jesus said, "Blessed are the peacemakers, for they shall be called sons of God" (Matt. 5:9). In the Latin Bible the word for peacemakers in this verse is *pacifici*, from which is formed directly the English term "pacifists," meaning literally those who make peace.

But the term "pacifism" has in our time become debased coin. It no longer signifies in popular usage what Jesus intended to say when He spoke His blessing on the peacemakers. He meant, we believe, to designate those persons, who, by teaching the gospel of Christ and by living the way Christ lived, bring about peaceful relations among people. They work to do away with strife and ill will through winning people to become followers of Christ, so that people will on the basis of personal religion forgive each other in cases of difficulty. In this sense the nonresistant believers are among the true pacifists or peacemakers.

Popular pacifism today, however, is something very different from what was indicated above as Scriptural pacifism. It is essentially a political or social philosophy, aiming at influencing national and international affairs and policies by any methods of propaganda or coercion short of violence and war. It engages in a direct attack on the institution of war and on the alleged causes of wars.

This pacifism is largely human idealism, based on a minimum of religious faith. It is humanistic rather than theistic or Biblical in its outlook. Because of this debased use of the term, non-resistant Christians avoid speaking of themselves as pacifists, though historically the name belongs to them more properly than to those who have unsurped and secularized it. Pacifism generally advocates reform through human efforts more than it does conversion through the grace and power of God.

52. IS PHYSICAL FORCE THE ONLY SUCCESSFUL MEANS OF OVERCOMING THE EVIL INTENTIONS OF UNREGENERATE PEOPLE?

The assertion is sometimes made that the only way to stop aggressors in some instances is through forcible resistance and violent restraint. Kindness, well-doing, and gentle reasoning, so we are told, may be right up to a certain point, but when these have no effect, then force must be employed.

This is not the Christian view at all. Christ did not teach nor practice any such doctrine. Suffering and not violent resistance is the final Christian answer to wicked aggressors, according to Christ.

To admit that physical resistance must be the final court of appeal in dealing with unregenerate men is in effect to deny the power of the Gospel of Jesus Christ. It is a fact, and one that has been verified many times by experience, that evil men have been won for Christ, have been turned from bad men into good men, and have been made from enemies into friends through the showing of love and good will. Violent resistance may sometimes overpower and subdue the other person; it never wins him to a better life or leads to his salvation. The Scriptural injunction is: "Be not overcome of evil, but overcome evil with good" (Romans 12:21). The context of this notable passage clearly suggests that the *good* is to be done to *enemies* to overcome their *evil* and that heaping coals of fire on the heads of enemies is the *good*. Of course, Paul did not mean to suggest that the way to overcome the world's evil (sin) is by deeds of kindness rather than by the saving work of Christ.

So far as nations are concerned, these cannot be nonresistant toward so-called aggressor nations for the simple reason that national policies based on years and centuries of self-interest and selfishness cannot be defended by nonresistant means. Nonresistance is compatible only with sacrificial living and unselfish well doing. War between nations is essentially God's judgment on the nations involved. Only God is wise enough to know what the aggressions of all the nations have been through the centuries, and He judges them for their sins by condemning them to engage in wars. The Christian should be separated from the selfish life of his nation, wherever he lives. He must be devoted to living a sacrificial life by the power of God. Only in so doing can he be consistently nonresistant in faith and practice. States and nations cannot be nonresistant until they become regenerate.

53. WHAT IS MEANT BY THE SEPARATION OF CHURCH AND STATE?

By the separation of church and state we understand that there is no organic connection between the two institutions. They operate in entirely different spheres, or on different levels. The church should not depend on the state for any part of its support or for promotion of its interests. Whatever the state sees fit to do for the church, as for instance in exempting church property from taxation, may be accepted by the church only so long as it implies no obligation on the part of the church to support the state in its policies and actions, or to become subservient in any way to it.

The state on its part must limit its activity to the secular and political sphere. It must not assume authority over the religious beliefs of the individual citizen, nor regulate what the church shall teach as regards religion, morals, and obedience to God.

Some Christian bodies teach that the individual citizen of the state, who is also a member of the church, must divide his loyalty between the two institutions, supporting each equally and in turn according to the demands made upon him. The nonresistant position is that the Christian owes supreme allegiance and loyalty to Jesus Christ, and that he must do what Christ asks him to do for the state or the nation in which he lives. Since the state uses force in carrying on many of its activities, nonresistant people have generally kept themselves aloof from participation in governmental functions, such as office-holding and political activity.

54. WHAT IS THE CHURCH'S PROPER TASK IN THE WORLD?

The church's proper task in the world is to represent Jesus Christ before the world. It is divinely commissioned to carry His Gospel of salvation to all nations, to make disciples of those who repent and believe, and to teach the believers to observe everything that Christ taught His disciples by word and by deed. This is the church's mission in the world as outlined by Christ before His ascension to heaven. See Matthew 28:18-20.

The church's task is not that of world reform. It is not commissioned to attack and correct existing social evils and injustice through political and coercive measures. Its work is not to try to force men and women to do right when they have in their hearts no desire to do right. Hence the church as such, and the members of the church, do not engage in political activity and in propaganda aimed purely at making a better society and a better world. Instead, they teach the Gospel and lead people to a new life through faith and conversion. They teach the Christian faith and ethic as there is opportunity, believing it to be the basis for all good moral and personal character, and they serve all men through well-doing in imitation of the Christ whom they confess as the Lord and Master of their life. They know that this is the only sure way to a better world.

55. IS THE CONSCIENTIOUS OBJECTOR WHO REFUSES TO DO MILITARY SERVICE OR PARTICIPATE IN WAR DISOBEDIENT TO THE GOVERNMENT AND DISLOYAL TO HIS COUNTRY?

Sometimes the charge is made that the conscientious objector, by refusing to accept military service, is disobedient to the government and disloyal to his country. This charge is made by those who are ignorant of the content of the present law governing military service, and its provisions for conscientious objectors. The Burke-Wadsworth Bill as passed in 1940 by the United States Congress, specifically provides in Section 5 (g) for complete exemption of sincere conscientious objectors from all military service, both combatant and non-combatant, provided they are found to be sincerely opposed by reason of religious training and belief to participation in war in any form. This act does provide for civilian service in lieu of military service, and specifically authorizes induction of conscientious objectors into "work of national importance under civilian direction," which service is altogether outside the jurisdiction of the armed forces in any form. Thus conscientious objectors who are adjudged sincere, and who accept induction into civilian service, fully discharge all their obligations to the government, and are in no wise disobedient or disloyal. Persons who question this should write to General Lewis B. Hershey, national director of Selective Service, Washington, D. C., for confirmation.

There is no other compulsion by law regarding national service in wartime than that provided by the Burke-Wadsworth Bill. All service in Civilian Defense work is purely voluntary. Likewise, there is no compulsion to buy war bonds. Most conscientious objectors of the nonresistant type are willing, glad, and ready to render service to the nation in wartime apart from official civilian defense organizations which ultimately have responsibility to the military authorities, and to purchase government bonds not designated as war bonds but intended to furnish funds for non-military, civilian needs of government which continue even during wartime. Nonresistant groups have never made trouble for their governments either in wartime or peace time, but are among the loyal, obedient, and sacrificial citizens of the lands. To class them with obstructionists, subverters, traitors, or enemies of the country, is possible only to those who are victims of ignorance, war hysteria, or deliberate perversion of the truth.

56. ARE THE MAJORITY OF THE DRAFTED CONSCIENTIOUS OB-
JECTORS IN THE PRESENT WAR NONRESISTANT, EVANGELICAL
BELIEVERS, OR ARE THEY HUMANITARIAN AND L I B E R A L
PACIFISTS?

Figures as of July 1, 1943, listing the denominational affili-
ation of all conscientious objectors drafted by the United States
Government into civilian public service "in work of national importance under civilian direction," show that a clear majority of
all these men are members of smaller thoroughly evangelical
denominations, concerning whose orthodoxy no question can be
raised. Approximately forty-one per cent are members of the
Mennonite and affiliated groups, another thirteen per cent are
members of the Church of the Brethren, and smaller numbers
members of other orthodox evangelical groups. This is not to say
that all of the remainder are theological liberals or belong to
churches which are liberal. There is no question about the evangelical and orthodox character of the majority of the "C.O.'s."

Dwight L. Moody and War

Reprinted from a tract published by the Middle District Conference of Mennonites, C. Henry Smith, Bluffton, Ohio, Editor.

The nineteenth century perhaps witnessed the greatest advance the Christian Church had ever known since the Reformation. Missions, education, and evangelism flourished and prospered. Great names emerged: Livingstone, Spurgeon, Booth, Finney, and Brooks. No name, however, loomed more mightily than that of Dwight L. Moody. From the depths of his great faith flowed a torrent of saving and cleansing triumphs. When he died in 1899, the greatest monuments to his divine labors were thousands of human beings in Europe and America who had experienced spiritual re-birth as a result of his God-inspired power.

Yet, it is a curious fact that with all this on-going publicity, the story of Dwight L. Moody as a *nonresistant* Christian is almost unknown. A careful reading of the official, authorized biography of the great evangelist written by his son, William R. Moody, reveals the full story.

Dwight L. Moody was a young man of 24, living in Chicago when the firing on Fort Sumter launched the tragic Civil War. Like all large cities, Chicago felt the excitement of this struggle; near the southern limits of the city Camp Douglas was started for the massing and instruction of recruits. Some of his own converts were among those who enlisted. Moreover, "a company was also raised among his friends and former associates in business, and on all sides he was urged to enter the service of his country."

His son points out that the cause of the Union appealed to the youthful Moody very strongly. For he had been an ardent abolitionist, having listened to the powerful oratory of men like William Lloyd Garrison, Wendell Philips, and Elijah P. Lovejoy. More amazing, his biographer-son records, were the public demonstrations against slavery in which he had joined.

But, in spite of all these heavy pressures toward the war, Dwight L. Moody could not enlist. Read his own words on the matter: *"There has never been a time in my life when I felt I could take a gun and shoot down a fellow being. In this respect I am a Quaker."* Precisely! This was the identical attitude of the Quakers, Mennonites, and Dunkards in the Civil War: Anti-slavery, pro-Union, but faithful to the commandment of Jesus Christ to ". . . Love your enemies, bless them that curse you, do good to them that hate you, and pray for them which despitefully use you and persecute you" (Matt. 5:44).

This conviction was maintained in his personal life. Once Moody was the silent spectator to a rather violent argument. To a friend he commented, *"Mac, the world is in great need of peace-makers."*

This conviction was also manifested in his preaching. One of his most famous sermons was called, "Good News." This tremendous message contains a famous passage which plumbs the very depths of forgiveness as taught by our Lord. Moody quotes Christ's famous farewell charge to His disciples: "Go ye into all the world, and preach the gospel to every creature." Then the imagination of the preacher is brought into the sermon. He imagines Peter saying, "Lord, do you really mean that we shall 'preach the gospel to every creature?' " The answer is, "Yes." Then Peter asks, "Shall we go back to those Jerusalem sinners who murdered you?" "Yes, Peter, go back there and tarry until you have been endued with power from on high. Offer the Gospel to them first. Go search the man who spat on my face; tell him I forgive him; there is nothing in my heart but love for him. Go search out the man who put that cruel crown of thorns on my brow; tell him that I will have a crown ready for him in my kingdom, if he will accept salvation; there shall not be a thorn in it, and he shall wear it forever and ever in the Kingdom of the Redeemer.

"Find out that man who took the reed from my hand and smote my head, driving the thorns deeper into my brow. If he will accept salvation as a gift, I will give him a scepter, and he shall have sway over the nations of the earth. Yes, I will give him to sit with me on my throne.

"Go seek that man who struck me with the palm of his hand; find him, and preach the Gospel to him; tell him that the blood of Jesus Christ cleanseth from all sin and my blood was shed for him freely.

"Go seek that soldier that drove the spear into my side; tell him there is a nearer way to my heart than that. Tell him that I forgive him freely; and tell him I will make him a soldier of the cross and my banner over him shall be love."

Here Dwight L. Moody has created a stirring picture of the Prince of Peace and His utter willingness to forgive seventy times seven; His compassionate love for those who do Him evil. *This* is the source of all true nonresistant testimony. Let us pray that God will raise up more true apostles of God's redeeming love like Dwight L. Moody.

A Short Bibliography on Non-resistance

A Brief Catechism on Difficult Scripture Passages and Involved Questions on the Use of the Sword............................P. H. Richert
Mennonite Publication Office, Newton, Kansas, 1942. 20 pp.

Applied Non-resistance..................................Peace Problems Committee
Mennonite Publishing House, Scottdale, Pa., 1939. 154 pp. Price 50c.

Can a Christian Fight...O. B. Ulery
E. V. Publishing House, Nappanee, Ind., 1942. 14 pp. Price 5c.

Can Christians Fight...G. F. Hershberger
Mennonite Publishing House, Scottdale, Pa., 1940. 180 pp. Price $1.25.

Christian Peace—Four Hundred Years of Mennonite Principles and Practice ....C. Henry Smith
Mennonite Publication Office, Newton, Kansas, 1938. 32 pp.

Christian Peace—New Testament Peace Teachings Outside the Gospel ....Ernest Bohn
Mennonite Publication Office, Newton, Kansas, 1938. 53 pp.

Die Biblische Lehre von der Wehrlosigkeit.......................John Horsch
Mennonite Publishing House, Scottdale, Pa., 1920. 127 pp. Price $1.00.

God and War...J. Irvin Lehman
Mennonite Publishing House, Scottdale, Pa., 1942. 63 pp. Price 20c.

Mennonites in the World War or Non-resistance Under Test ....J. S. Hartzler
Mennonite Publishing House, Scottdale, Pa., 1921. 246 pp. Price $1.00.

Nonresistance and the State....................................G. F. Hershberger
Mennonite Publishing House, Scottdale, Pa., 1935. 48 pp. Price 10c.

Non-resistance in Colonial Pennsylvania ....W. J. Bender
Mennonite Publishing House, Scottdale, Pa., 1934. 32 pp. Price 15c.

Non-resistance in Practice..J. S. Hartzler
Mennonite Publishing House, Scottdale, Pa., 1930. 47 pp. Price 10c.

Non-resistance Under Test ....E. J. Swalm
E. V. Publishing House, Nappanee, Ind., 1938. 55 pp. Price 25c.

Peace Principles ....Edward Yoder
Mennonite Publishing House, Scottdale, Pa. 32 pp. Price 5c.

Scriptural Basis of the Principles of Non-resistance and Christian Love ....David V. Wiebe
Salem Publishing House, Inman, Kansas, 1940. 80 pp.

Should God's People Partake in War....................................T. H. Epp
Salem Publishing House, Inman, Kansas, 1938. 25 pp. Price 10c.

Symposium on War..John Horsch
Mennonite Publishing House, Scottdale, Pa., 1927. 44 pp. Price 10c.

The Principle of Non-resistance as Held by the Mennonite Church ....John Horsch
Mennonite Publishing House, Scottdale, Pa., 1927-1939. 60 pp. Price 10c.

War and the Christian Conscience ....John Horsch
Mennonite Publishing House, Scottdale, Pa., 1930. 16 pp. Price 2c.

War—Peace—Amity ....H. P. Krehbiel
Mennonite Publication Office, Newton, Kans., 1937. 350 pp. Price $2.00.

War, Peace, and Non-resistance................................G. F. Hershberger
Mennonite Publishing House, Scottdale, Pa., 1943. 450 pp. Price $1.50.